BUILD YOUR CREATIVE BUSINESS THE HEARTIZAN WAY

Where hearts, crafts and minds meet for success

CHRISSIE LOWERY

Heartizan

CONTENTS

Build Your Business The Heartizan Way

First published in the United Kingdom in 2019 by Heartizan Media

https://heartizan.uk.com

ISBN 9781689959513

Cover design, photography, illustrations and graphics: Mollie Phillips

Wreath Image: Bernadette Rosenquest – Unique Handcrafted Chic

Additional photography: Lisa Lucas LRPS, Lisa Lucas Photography

Project management, structural editing, marketing guidance: Suzan St Maur

Copy & line editing: Andrew Lowe

Book production: Helen Stothard

FOREWORD BY JULES WHITE

I can't fail but admire the incredible skills, talents and patience demonstrated in this remarkable book about hand crafting.

Not only is it about exploring and exposing some unbelievable talents in using simple items to create works of art, like book folding, for example. How intricate and delicate is that? But also there are so many other ways in which people express their creativity.

In this stunning book by Chrissie Lowery she shares just what unbelievably complex and intricate artefacts these hand crafting skills can become, be appreciated for, and be turned into businesses.

What's even more fascinating is that here, she captures the stories of dozens of people for whom hand crafting -- if a hobby to begin with -- not only has become a business opportunity: it also has become a personal lifesaver.

Her tagline mentions "where hearts, crafts and minds meet for success." I'd say that's a pretty good summary of everything this book represents.

Chrissie is a total inspiration and is always helping people who might previously have thought of themselves as 'hobbyists' ... by providing them with a platform that can spur them on into higher echelons of small business and beyond. Not just a platform I might add, but a community and total support network. She has created something very special indeed and this book is yet another way for us to really appreciate the magic and beauty of crafting.

Jules White
Multi-award winning international sales coach,
"Dragons' Den" winner, TEDx speaker,
author, *Live It, Love It, Sell It.*

SOME THANKS

Over the years the people that I have connected with have suggested that I write a book, but until now I haven't wanted to share my story, so I would like to thank them for having faith in me!

I wish to thank all the Heartizan Creatives that inspire me every single day. I would also like to thank all the wonderful people, business owners, coaches, my Madmin team, my brother and of course my children for helping me create something that truly makes a difference.

Dad, I thank you the most; you always believed in me and encouraged me that I could do anything and be anyone!

Chrissie

INTRODUCTION

Crafting can be great therapy, or a hobby and even for family time but if you are creating to make money it can also be a lonely, scary, isolative and non-profitable learning curve. We ask our friends their opinions and we hang out in crafting groups to try and learn; we all want to succeed and ultimately sell our creations! This book is to help you grow, save you money and to be used as a reference when help is needed, and you don't know where to turn. I have written this book in an informal and conversational way so that absorbing its contents is easy and manage- able. It is like a patchwork quilt of personal stories, shared experiences, inspirational gems and powerful business advice from someone who really has walked the walk and came out the other side!

There have been times when I felt the worst Mum in the world, when I have been on my phone or my laptop working and I haven't really been there for my children. Getting the right work/home balance is difficult and trying to juggle everything is part of being a small business owner. I can only hope that I am a good role model to my children, they are very proud of me and they do get involved with my businesses.

Being a sole trader, entrepreneur or even part of a limited company is not an easy role but I would not change it and I love working for myself.

I do get a lot of inspiration from my children, my friends, my Madmins and my fabulous creatives, all of whom go through their own challenges and hard times.

An amazing team helps to run Heartizan and one very lovely lady Dolly (Angela Ramsden) has helped me collate our creative stories and has kept me accountable, for which I am very grateful. I get easily distracted with Heartizan, being pulled here, there and everywhere.

This book will guide creatives who have been on a similar business journey, walked in my footsteps and need a helping hand; a cry; a friend and even a crafting family that really understands them.

Heartizan is so much more than a marketplace, it is the heart and soul of an amazing community! The creatives of Heartizan are incredible people and they truly are like family. We help each other, we learn together, and we support each other. My team work tirelessly and even put our creatives before their own businesses and are worth their weight in gold.

CRAFT, DRUGS AND MEMORY PROBLEMS

I was placed on sick leave for a year before I had to give up my career. Being a Clinical Nurse Specialist was all I had ever dreamed of – even as a child, I wanted to be a nurse. My family life and work balance was just how I liked it. I had worked on a Psychiatric Intensive Care Unit and as a Specialist Nurse in the Youth Support Team. I have always worked in the care sector and helping people was second nature to me, it was in my genes! My mum had been a Marie Curie nurse and when she was younger, she ran an older adult unit. My work history varied from the care sector to a mechanic and to running a shop! Before I embarked on my nursing career, I managed a home for adults with autism and I have had many jobs in this field, including working with people with learning disabilities and for the Special Education Service in New Zealand.

When I became unwell, I was not sure what to do with myself. I became lost and isolated. I made my son his first 'Snugglebed' (I have rebranded since this time) and his sleep improved dramatically. We finally stopped being a sleep deprived family and I found a purpose and a focus in my life (see Chapter 9 for my story).

My new friends from the many support groups I joined were people who had all been on the same journey as me. I started to discover what was wrong with me: it turned out that I'm what is known as a "spoonie", or someone who suffers from chronic illness. My particular illnesses include fibromyalgia, pernicious anaemia, spinal problems and osteoarthritis but I have lots of 'bonus' ones too.

Looking back, I had lots of symptoms, but I put them down to different things: too much driving for work, stress and not looking after myself properly. I was very fit, I juggled a stressful career which I loved; however, the paperwork was becoming excessive, especially with me being a single parent to my five children plus two (now three) grandsons. My first grandson was born just three weeks before my youngest son; they are now 11, 8 and 2 years old.

At my worst, I forgot how to operate my car and I began to see colours blurring in front of me. I have minimal memories of this time; however a few remain in my head. I called my mechanic after dropping my children off at football practice as my car would not start, or so I thought. It was an automatic car and I had forgotten that it had to be in Park while pressing the brake pedal. I forgot this on two occasions. I did not pick my children up on time one day and was over an hour late; I did not know where I had been. I left money in the cash machine on several occasions and then my memory really deteriorated. I could not remember when my children were born, the times and their weights or even their early years and I began to lose much larger chunks of my memory.

I quickly learnt that everyone had an opinion on memory issues; they all had them and said they "knew what I meant" but I was not forgetful – I had a pathological memory disorder. I had forgotten major life events as well as the little quotidian things.

So, I was tested and scanned as the medical team wanted to rule out ovarian or bowel cancer. I was referred to a lot of specialists and I ended up having two operations. My friends were very supportive initially and so were the close members of my family.

My hands, face and feet were numb, I was too ill to work, I couldn't sleep and running my home was impossible. The rest of that year was a blur to me, but eventually I was diagnosed and I tried to move forward.

I somehow set up a Facebook page, though I don't remember doing it. I had created a product from my son's sleep problems and I had found a solution. As a family, we had been desperate for sleep, so I decided to help other families like mine, so my children and I made lots of Snugglebedz. I sold them on local Facebook selling sites and I found that people loved them, which helped me to start rebuilding my life again.

However, my health continued to deteriorate and the next year I was diagnosed with fibromyalgia, carpal tunnel, arthritis, chronic fatigue and chronic pain syndrome. I was given many different kinds of medication and I started to gain weight.

In the following year, I was diagnosed with a memory disorder and was given referrals to the pain clinic and even more drugs! The pain clinic was a half-hour drive and driving was becoming painful. I had to sit in a room for over two hours, which was uncomfortable, and things hurt too much to sit for that length of time. The staff were fabulous, but I couldn't complete the sessions. I was given help on chronic fatigue syndrome; how to manage pain and a TENS machine. I had nerve conduction tests; x-rays; MRIs and other scans. The year after, I had an operation for carpal tunnel syndrome, was diagnosed with greater pain syndrome and my hip was treated with electric therapy. I started physio and was referred to the MSKAT team. There they x-rayed my neck and told me I probably had crushed neck syndrome. My health issues appeared to be ongoing and I realised they would probably never change.

I have had to learn to pace myself and rest when I need to. I knew that I was not employable anymore and that took quite some time to come to terms with.

I would struggle to get through the days which would at times, also affect my children. To live a different way takes a lot of retraining and learning how to achieve things when you have limitations. It starts with acceptance which isn't easy and like most people with chronic illnesses I made a lot of mistakes, but I also learnt how to live with them and move on, even with a smile on some occasions!

When you are chronically ill, you soon find out who really loves you and who will stick by you, no matter what. You lose family, friends and partners because you aren't the same person you once were. I worked on my relationships, I wore my heart on my sleeve, I showed up and the important people in my life meant the world to me. I quickly found out that this was not reciprocated and when I didn't manage to get out of bed for nights out, lunches, or even to answer the phone, it became clear who my friends were.

I don't have the social life or friendship network that I used to have before becoming unwell, but I know for sure that the few friends I have left care and support me and will always be in my life, no matter what. I would like to thank two very special ladies who have never judged me, let me down or belittled me. You know who you are, and I will always be truly thankful.

I do not remember most of the early business years, from having the seed in my mind to actually creating a business, but I do have my photos. One important thing that I have learnt through this journey is to record everything! Take a lot of photos, take them of your works in progress, your events, networking, wins and not so good times. Take photos of your family, children, pets and even your friends. Most phone cameras will date the images and when you come to look back and reuse/repurpose them this will be so helpful.

Even though I had not set up my business at this point and I had a lot of struggles to get through for my children. Their school was not supportive of extra needs and I had to find them an alternative educational setting.

I knew that I had a good business idea and it felt that everything that had happened had been pointing me in this direction.

The twins settled in at their new school, but my youngest son started to struggle; his previous experience of schools made him distrustful of teachers and the bullying had affected him a lot more than I had thought. He couldn't relate well to the other children and he became sad and isolated. My heart started to break all over again and I found it very difficult to stay focused on my plans. Even though I knew this was the right direction for me, my son had to come first. I muddled through but my family life was taking a beating and I found it very hard to keep my dreams alive. Transitioning from a career woman to a business owner was also a tough journey and you have to continue to believe in yourself. I found myself following inspirational speakers and learning how they overcame their hardships, which in turn helped me overcome my fears, step into my 'power' which helped me to let go of the past and move on.

HEARTIZAN - HOW TO OVERCOME HARDSHIPS AND CHASE YOUR DREAMS

- **Believe in yourself!**
- Let go of what has happened to you – leave that past behind you.
- Find your power (what it is that you represent or what you want to be known for).
- Get help if you need it – find a professional who can help you move on.
- Set goals and make plans; make your dreams happen.
- Find your why (what lights you up, why you are creating your products and what keeps you doing it).
- Use your why to keep going.
- Avoid blaming yourself – it will stop you from moving forward.
- Be patient, business is a marathon and not a sprint.
- Talk and talk more; tell your partner, friends and colleagues what your plans are, they will support you.
- Control any angry thoughts or feelings you may have; these are normal but don't let them spill from your brain and come out of your mouth.

- Help each other; helping solve problems for others will also help you.
- Try to reduce your stress.
- Believe that the best is yet to come.
- Find inspiration and motivation.
- Practise your craft and practise some more.
- Be kind to yourself, try not to listen to that self-critic and have faith in yourself.
- Try a change of environment, work somewhere different, spend time decluttering.
- Find people that you can connect with, reach out and start surrounding yourself with positive trailblazers.

Lastly, take risks, go outside your comfort zone, feel the fear and do it anyway

These inspirational speakers and public figures that I have followed are some of the key people who have helped me through the dark times. I read their books, watched their lives, speeches, talks and write-ups:

- Will Smith
- Theo Paphitis
- Keanu Reeves
- Oprah
- Muhammad Ali
- Richard Branson
- Michael Jordan
- Hellen Keller
- Lady Gaga
- Walt Disney
- Tony Robbins
- Jim Carrey
- Emma Watson.

BUNTING AND BUSINESS PLANS

After that dark year I began to realise that I would not be able to go back to my nursing career. I was too unwell and I could not get through the day without experiencing a lot of pain, sleep disruption and some very strange symptoms. Many people with chronic illnesses start creating to distract them from pain and to give them a reason to get up in the morning. Crafting kind of just found me and it solved a problem for my family. I am really not sure how those early business start- up plans formed in my head, but I am sure that everything happens for a reason.

I was sent an appointment to go into my local job centre to see a lady called Sarah, who specialised in illness, diagnoses and benefits. I will never forget how much she helped me and how she was such an inte- gral cog in setting up my business. Before meeting Sarah, I had no plans of how to make my hobby into a proper business. However, the children were now all in school and I needed to feel like I was getting back to normal by having some direction, goals and dreams. My youngest son was on a reduced timetable, but this was increasing and I had a huge need to be working again.

I joined our local enterprise scheme, through Sarah's recommendation and I was assigned an amazing mentor. Adrian helped me to write a business plan and he guided me through the set-up steps of launching my own business. I was not allowed to trade for the next twelve weeks but I did make products and started a launch campaign. I also applied to Dragons Den (which in hindsight was far too early but a great experience).

We researched playgroups, nurseries and school groups to promote my cuddle beds and cushions. I had a new direction and my whole persona and outlook on life changed. I felt the old me returning and I felt happy again. During the next few months, we contacted many establishments and I learnt a lot about face-to-face business. I also started to learn about what being a business owner really meant. You have to juggle a lot of hats, invest a lot of time and money to grow and surround your-self with like-minded people. When I was allowed to trade again, I started to look into other social media options and selling platforms along with planning my own website. At the time, I was only selling on Facebook and I knew I had to find other selling platforms.

I started to share my story and a local newspaper came to interview me. They published my journey and introduced me to their marketing manager and things began to change. After my story appeared in the newspaper, I had large orders from schools and nurseries and I grew my range, adding cushions and garden products. I decided to pay for a website, but this was a huge learning curve and I had to go through a few developers until I found the right one.

I was then nominated for some local business awards. I was judged to be a recommended local business and listed as among the top 21 busi-nesses to watch out for in the future. I had a purpose, a reason to get dressed and face each day and I started to feel the grief for my old life start to ebb away. As I grew, so did my fabric stash and my equipment; I didn't have my own craft room, as my house was small, and my busi-ness was taking over. My supplies were spread everywhere, and we could not move without being covered in fluff and threads. I stashed fabrics in cupboards and pillows were piled high.

I decided to rent a corner of a pet shop and I finally felt that my little business was growing. Not having the whole business in my house was so much better and I could start to create a life/work balance. I was no longer crafting on the floor, I had stock and a work space that I was very proud of!

I then got a phone call from Dragons' Den calling me in for an audition – I was on a shortlist of three hundred people, taken from three thousand. Sadly, that was as far as it went but it was an amazing experience. They did not give me much time to prepare, only a few days, and I had to learn a pitch, make some amazing products and drive to London with my friend. It took me around 12 takes until we were all finally happy and my pitch then went to the producers along with my promotional material and my products. I had not even started to trade and my business was being mentored in preparation to sell my products whilst I worked on my plans with my mentor. I did not get through to the next stage of Dragons' Den, but I was proud to have been short- listed and a few weeks later I launched my very first business.

I have now been featured in other papers and online sites. I started networking and meeting other sole traders, learning from them and growing each month. I began to learn how Facebook really worked and I grew my followers and used the same social media platforms for all my sales and connections. I also reached out to experts and invested in some courses, including Facebook Live. I knew my story was a big part of my business and I needed to find a way of sharing it with a larger audience. I discovered Stacy Sargison, who at the time ran a group called JFDI. I watched her live videos and I interacted in her group and started making some connections with other businesses. I completed a Facebook Live course a few months later and this really changed the way I thought about business, my confidence and my personal life. The course was amazing and by the end of it I was hooked on lives. I also knew that I needed more help with my business, so I joined a local networking group called StroudNet. This event is run by a fantastic coach, Robin Waite, who really helped me upscale my business and teach me strategies and how to approach larger companies to sell wholesale and drop ship.

I worked with Robin for a year and I learnt so much more than how to run a business: I learnt the theory and the core elements of all successful businesses.

At the same time, I was running an online networking group with other crafters all trying to gain exposure and make sales. This is where Heartizan really started. Even the networking group had potential to grow and be monetised. I had admins who helped run the group, which then became three groups and a page. At the beginning of my journey I applied for a well-known marketplace to sell my Cuddle Beds. I was rejected but the seed was sown – I would one day build my own!

That year I also entered a competition called Dragonesses' Den which is very similar to the TV show, however you have to pitch to a live audience. All my fears and lack of confidence started to bubble up again. Robin helped me to prepare for the Den and I learnt how to breathe and deliver a speech. The live streaming also helped, and I could now really pitch my business! I had a few stages to go through, but I somehow passed through them and before I knew it I was on stage pitching to a live audience and three dragonesses. This was probably the scariest thing I have ever done. I was incredibly nervous and, even though I practised a lot, I was not ready for the big day. My friends came with me for support and Robin was there too, but I had to wait until the afternoon and my anxiety went through the roof. My gorgeous friend, who had been on my business journey from the beginning, was there by my side whilst I carried out my pitch.

It was very similar to Dragons' Den and I had to do an elevator pitch but mostly to the audience in front of me. I managed to get though it and then there were questions and deliberations, but I had won! The feeling was amazing, and my confidence soared! I learnt so much from the Women's Club that year along with my coaching sessions with Robin. Investment is such a large part of growing your business.

Later that year, I discovered Twitter. I am not sure how I did this because at the time I did not understand it, I had no clue what it was for! My daughter used Twitter and showed me the basics, so I started to navigate my way around it.

I found some creative hours to join Small Business Sunday (SBS), run by Theo Paphitis (Dragons Den) amongst others. When I applied to Dragons' Den, I watched every single episode and I loved Theo and his story, so I started to tweet him each and every week. Small Business Sunday is a great boost to any business and I started to set reminders on my phone so that I would not miss out on a chance to win.

I tweeted various texts and images each Sunday but when I checked on the following Monday when Theo announced the winners, I wasn't successful. I didn't give up and I made sure I tweeted each week even though Sunday evenings are a little busy in my household.

The night before I won SBS, I tweeted Theo about my Cuddle Beds and how they could help people with extra needs, disorders and disabilities. On Monday evening I was putting the children to bed when my phone went crazy! It was in my back pocket when the pings started. I was saying goodnight to the children and, at first, I had no idea what was happening. I checked my phone and there was my tweet being retweeted everywhere and it dawned on me that I had won SBS so we all did a happy dance! I kissed my children goodnight and I spent the rest of the evening answering everyone's congratulations. This lasted a few days, along with the #SBSwinnershour the following day.

It was my first Twitter award and I was absolutely thrilled. I was then given a press release, a logo, a banner and I set up my shop on Theo Paphitis marketplace. All winners get the opportunity to attend the SBS event where the winners receive their award from the man himself. This boost for my business was just what I needed; my presence on Twitter grew and I started making connections with fellow business owners. I have developed quite a business crush on Theo over the years when he was a Dragon and I love the golden nuggets and words of wisdom that he shares with his SBS winners. He is such a great ambassador for people like me and the support I have received though Small Business Sunday, the crew, the SBS family, new friends and Theo himself has been incredible.

I would highly recommend Small Businesses to tweet Theo on a Sunday between 5pm and 7.30pm as it's a game changer!

HERE IS MY WINNING TWEET:

@TheoPaphitis my sensory Cuddle Beds are helping children with ASD and sensory needs to sleep better. We are working on a new model too! I also added four product images.

With my new-found confidence and my coach Robin keeping me accountable, I started to contact various newspapers, magazines and charities. I contacted the National Autistic Society and they featured me in their magazine. I contacted wholesalers and Wayfair accepted me as a seller – everything suddenly started to happen. Orders were rolling in for Cuddle Beds and I didn't have time to even launch my new products. I was on BBC Radio, Forbes, The International Story Exchange and many others. I had an amazing Golden Quarter (the last quarter of the year) – Christmas is where most retail businesses make the most money!

After Christmas, I prepared for Theo's Small Business Sunday event, which was an incredible experience. I was so excited and I signed up to everything that landed in my inbox. My friend and I booked a fabulous hotel which was connected to the International Conference Centre and when we arrived, I felt just like an excited tourist! There were lots of stands giving out freebies and the centre was fabulous! I was a mixed bag of emotions, overwhelmed and I had no real sense of direction or how to take my business up to the next level. However, standing among so many small business owners, I felt an immediate change in me. I was surrounded by like-minded people who lifted me up and inspired me and for the first time I actually felt like the "Super Mum" that my friends often called me.

I had a plan of action for the day and I had made a connection with a fabulous business owner who I had connected with on Twitter.

Dylan Moore really helped me learn and grow on Twitter and still continues to support Heartizan in all aspects of business. He is a fellow SBS winner and has a massive wealth of knowledge on all things Twitter related. I am very lucky to have his support for both of my businesses. I had signed up to a couple of pitches at the event and the first one was due to start not long after we arrived. I was informed that the junior buyer from Robert Dyas was looking for me, his name was Lloyd and he told me that Cuddle Beds were the only business that they were interested in that day. I wasn't nervous beforehand but when I realised how real this was, I began to freak out a little! I tried to keep myself calm and I delivered a good pitch, but I could see the senior buyers knew I was not ready for such a huge scale up.

The whole day was amazing and I implemented the rest of my plan for the event. I met wonderful people and then queued to receive my award from Theo. We couldn't talk to Theo in advance as there were so many of us, however having my photo taken with him with one of my products was a huge opportunity in itself and by the end of the day I was absolutely flying. I had listened to incredibly inspiring people who had been on similar paths to my own and I took away so much from each and every one of them. Theo had an amazing presence and his positive, down to earth approach was infectious. I was lucky enough to have my questions answered and right at the end of the event when most people had gone home, I also took a selfie with him.

My journey with Theo did not stop there and I am now selling my products in his Robert Dyas online shop. I made this happen by contacting the senior buyer on LinkedIn and by sending two of my beanbags to their headquarters. I learnt a huge amount. Drop shipping and wholesaling is not easy to set up but now I understand the process and having this extra revenue stream and being a trusted seller of Robert Dyas is brilliant for my business.

I did have some challenges though, and the next one was my business name. I applied to The Intellectual Property Office to trademark my business name and protect my Cuddle Beds.

This is a straight forward process and my protection was in place fairly quickly, however the trademark was not so easy. Once you fill in all your details, the submission is entered in the trade magazine for two months to give an opportunity for it to be opposed. At this time, I was Snugglebedz, and unfortunately it was opposed, and I had to seek legal help. Even though my trademark was different in design and wording, another company was not happy that I had applied and they sent me many threatening letters. I did not understand but the legal team explained that even though I could win in court, it would cost thousands of pounds. I would also not be allowed to trade in the months before the case was heard. It became very complicated and I was given the trademark for selling pet products only.

I made the decision to change my business name to 'The Cuddle Bed Company' with the help of a technique from Robin Waite; this technique was also used for Heartizan. I had a logo designed for me and I am now trademarked.

I was introduced to Carlo Buschetto, a businessman from Indishor Productions, who not only helped me with my Twitter account but made fabulous videos too. We discussed my plans and how I wanted to expand my sensory ranges. He knew a lot about football clubs and researched ones with sensory rooms. I added these to my spreadsheet, and I made contact with Notts County and Tottenham Hotspur.

I won more awards on Twitter and was now an official multi-award-winning business! I started building up relationships, reached out to bloggers and I had my Cuddle Beds reviewed online for me.

This is a blog post from Hayley Beth who can be found on Twitter, Facebook and on her own website – Love Hayley Beth

"Welcome to a brand-new series of blogs whereby I get to introduce you to fantastic businesses and tell you their story. Now I must warn you this post is about an incredibly inspirational woman whose story might just bring you to tears. She has a brilliant positive attitude and doesn't let anything get in her way.

Introducing Chrissie Lowery

Like many people, Chrissie lived a perfectly normal life, a career in care managing residential homes for adults with autism that then evolved into a career in nursing working in a Psychiatric Intensive Care Unit at Wotton Lawn for five years. She then went on to work as a Clinical Nurse Specialist with the Youth Support Team. But all of this started to change after falling pregnant with her beautiful twins. At about five months into the pregnancy, Chrissie was admitted to hospital with liver failure. Shortly after this, Amber had decided she was ready for this world and she popped on out. Zack wasn't quite ready, happily curled up in the warmth. Not wanting a caesarean, this tiny boy was given a little encouragement and eventually he graced the world with his presence.

Due to their early birth, the twins were incubated, and it was quickly realised they were not well. At six weeks old they were diagnosed with CMV, a virus that can be deadly for unborn babies. It was too late to treat them. They subsequently spent three months in intensive care. Fast forward to 2013 and her twins are living happy healthy lives. They even have a little brother too. This is the year the story really begins. All three children are at the local village school and the eldest boy gets dubbed the 'naughty kid' and is diagnosed with autism and the youngest is getting severely bullied. If this wasn't enough, Chrissie falls ill with chronic illness causing her to spend many days in bed and on the sofa. The only thing she could do is pull the children out of school and educate them at home. At this point, her eldest son hadn't been

21

sleeping great and Chrissie, having plenty of time at home, discovered this great world of the internet!!! After doing a bit of research, she found a basic version of what she now calls a Cuddle Bed. Sat on the floor in her living room with her mum's old sewing machine, she taught herself how to sew and so the first Cuddle Bed was made. Since that day her son has always slept through the night. Chrissie now has the IPO rights to her design.

I guess you could say that was Chrissie's lightbulb moment. She then went on to make her other children and grandsons one and she thought to herself "you know what, I quite enjoy this." On the off chance that others might like the look of them she posted them onto a couple of for sale and wanted groups on everybody's favourite, Facebook. I guess you could say it exploded with friends and family members all wanting one.

It was then found Chrissie had a B12 deficiency, arthritis, malabsorption syndrome, fibromyalgia and carpal tunnel syndrome. She had to give up work. This is something she has come to terms with in the last few months. Needing help and direction, Chrissie took part in the Gloucestershire Enterprise Scheme. She travelled around the southwest visiting schools and nurseries introducing herself and Cuddle Beds. Due to being on this scheme she wasn't allowed to make any money off of the beds made for these establishments, but it gave her a wealth of experience and she learnt so much valuable information.

The next business step was renting the corner of a local pet shop. All three children were now back in mainstream education and her eldest son was getting the support he really needed. In the coming months, Chrissie focused her energies into making Cuddle Beds a success. She auditioned for Dragons' Den (although not successful at the time, she has been asked to try again) and created her own Facebook page and her first website.

Her twins were featured in Forbes magazine in a Facebook Live video and Chrissie also won Dragonesses' Den, a brilliant accolade for a great businesswoman. Chrissie also hired a business coach who has *helped her find confidence in recording Facebook Live videos amongst many other things. The whole reason she made her first Cuddle Bed was to help her son. In light of this, Chrissie contacted The National Autistic Society and had a brilliant article written.*

She gained a lot of interest from parents of autistic children and was able to do what she really wanted: to help people. The article also caught the eye of Catherine Bailey, Creator of Parents in Need, who has since added the Cuddle Beds link to the Parents in Need website. She then moved out of the corner of that pet shop and moved into an actual unit! She got invited to an event for amazing women and had the chance to meet Patsy Palmer. She won Theo Paphitis Small Business Sunday, meaning she can now sell her products through his exclusive site.

In the last week, her trademark came through, making Cuddle Beds completely hers. But what I think is really amazing is that on the very day that Chrissie got in contact with me she had her story published on The Story Exchange. I felt incredibly honoured to know that despite all of that she wanted to meet me and let me tell her story. What really grabbed my attention was not only what she has already accomplished but her dream and her one true goal. It had always been to help people. To do this she has come up with the idea to create a sensory Cuddle Bed. The idea is that each Sensory Bed will vary depending on the child it is for, with different fabrics, scents, sounds and even lights!"

This review is from a fellow SBS winner Georgina Durrant who writes "The Special Educational Needs Resources Blog" which can be found on Twitter, Facebook and her own website

"Sleep is the holy grail in parenting circles. Having children who don't sleep well not only affects the child but can impact on their whole family. Whether it be children struggling to get to sleep, waking in the

night or getting up too early – it can be incredibly difficult to cope with for any parent. It can be a challenge that all families can experience, but sleep problems are particularly prevalent for children with special educational needs. I was therefore thrilled to discover The Cuddle Bed Company".

Founded by Chrissie Lowery, a mum of five, The Cuddle Bed Company designs and makes Cuddle Beds, bean bags and cushions for all children with a particular focus on helping those with Special Educational Needs. Chrissie's Cuddle Beds are inspired by her autistic son. She began making Cuddle Beds for her son to help him sleep better; catering for his need for sensory stimulation. We tried out a Toddler Cuddle Bed, which is designed to be a temporary bed for chil-dren over the age of 2."

What did we like about them?

Relaxing*: We think they are a brilliant idea to help children who get overstimulated and need a safe and comfortable place to relax, or for those who need sensory stimulation to settle. In terms of sensory stimu-lation, the Cuddle Beds are appropriately named as you almost sink inside them, it's like you're being cuddled by cushions! Focusing on how lying on the Cuddle Bed feels helps children (and adults) to feel safe and less stimulated by other things around them.*

Multiple Uses: *The Cuddle Bed range caters for toddlers, children and teenagers. The beds have numerous uses, such as for sleepovers, camp-ing, relaxing, reading, watching TV, playing games etc. We found ours to be really handy for our toddler's nap times and as a lovely place for our children to snuggle with books to relax before bedtime. We are also looking forward to trying it out when we stay with family.*

High quality: *They've used 100% Cotton or Polycotton top fabrics, the designs are stunning, and the beds are beautifully made to a high stan-dard. The care, love and attention to detail that Chrissie Lowery puts into each of the beds is wonderful.*

Options: *On The Cuddle Bed Company's website there is a very wide* *range of beautiful fabric pattern and colours to choose from to customise a bed for your child. I loved this feature, as in my experience, children are more likely to use and love a product that they have helped to customise/choose.*

Practical*: I adored the practicality of the Cuddle Bed. It folds up easily (unlike sleeping bags!) into its own bag and is secured neatly with a drawstring, helping it to be tidied away/stored or transported, for example to grandparents' houses. It's also lightweight and easy to carry. Plus, the top cover is washable, so there's no worries with removing spillages.*

HEARTIZAN - HOW TO SET UP YOUR BUSINESS

- Reach out to your local connections to see if you can have a blog written about you or have your products reviewed, like the ones at the end of this chapter.
- Follow Journo requests and Haro on Twitter – there are a lot of bloggers, journalists and other businesses looking to share stories.
- Business name – check to see if your domain name is available, try somewhere like 123 Reg and buy it even if you don't plan on using it. Carry out more research, check the Intellectual Property Office – Google and look on Facebook.
- HMRC – get yourself registered; this is a legal requirement (this does vary on turnover but is subject to change).
- Social Media Platforms – set up accounts on Facebook, LinkedIn, Twitter, YouTube, Instagram and Pinterest – there are others, but these are a good start, however you don't really need to be everywhere all of the time and you will find the best platforms that suit your business.
- Target Audience – find out who would buy your products, track your sales and find out where they hang out (Facebook groups, magazines/papers they read etc).

- Mailchimp – set up an account – you don't have to have a website.
- Blog account – if you don't have a website, this is a great way to get seen – there are free ones that you can access.
- Join Facebook groups and get visible, share your stories and products (not in a salesy way).
- Sell your products on a sales platform, Heartizan is the best one I know!
- Link your Facebook page to your listing and to your Heartizan shop.
- Make it easy for your customers to find your products and buy with one or two clicks.
- Keep your social media page updated, you should ideally post three times a day but also test what the interaction is and what times are best for your business.
- Engage your audience – always reply to comments, ask questions, beta test and set polls on your pages.
- Make sure you take your photos on a white background so they are clear to identify and potential customers can see them clearly. We are a scrolling nation and there are a lot of creative businesses, make sure your images stand out.
- Consider going live, this really does help not only your reach but your confidence also. If you wish to scale up your business, confidence is the key!
- Push yourselves outside of your comfort zone, if you keep on doing the same thing you will get the same results!
- Network with other crafters, have conversations so people remember and connect with you. Know your why! To really understand your target audience, you need to understand yourself and why you are doing what you do.
- Think about the problem that you are solving for your customers and tailor your marketing to fixing it for them.
- Buy Robin Waite's book – Online Business Start Up.
- Buy Jules White's book – Live It, Love It, Sell It –join her group, watch her TEDx talk and listen to her podcasts.

- Follow Ed Troxell Creative on his Facebook page and sign up for his newsletter, check out his website.
- Take great images, this is so important and maybe invest in a good camera or a light box.
- Contact your local newspaper or even the radio station to make connections with them and to start your storytelling.

CRAFTINESS IS HAPPINESS

The Heartizan page ran for a year before we launched the website. I struggled with running the group, my business and my pages so the marketplace was put on the back burner. One of the ladies who I had asked to help had to leave so I concentrated on my Cuddle Beds. I now had the IP design rights so no one could copy my designs as they were registered and protected with the Intellectual Property Office. I then started expanding my range and added beanbags, blankets, cushions and accessories. My trademark was approved and I now had all the foundations to build a successful business.

At this stage, I thought I knew quite a lot about business, but I was wrong! I am a workaholic and hard work is nothing new to me, but launching a marketplace was an incredible amount of work. It affected my health and my energy was gone much quicker than it used to be nearly every day. Christmas time was spent in bed, still working on the social media side of both businesses, but this was very limited. The next few months I learnt a lot about websites, how they worked and what the front and back ends were! I met with the developers, had training sessions and set up lots of accounts to link in with the site.

What I learned in a few short months was incredible. My website was built by a fabulous business called Anorak Cat which is run by Rich and Amy, I had little knowledge of anything apart from being able to list a product, I was a total technophobe! I would recommend checking out your developer, looking at websites they have built and reading reviews too; you can spend a lot of money on a website and getting it right is so important. Rich can be found on social media and of course on his own website too.

Without my team and the amazing people I had met on the way, I would never have been able to launch Heartizan. Ed Troxell from America gave me invaluable advice; he is a tech god so I learnt how to use technology to grow Heartizan and to do it in an authentic way. I realised my knowledge on sales was limited (for a marketplace) and I needed help, so I invested in an amazing sales coach called Jules White. We had connected on Facebook and I had seen her fabulous pitch on Dragons' Den years before. One is just drawn to some people and in my business journey there are a few this has happened with, including Jules. I met with Jules and told her all about Heartizan and asked if she could help us, which of course she could. Having someone to keep you accountable and to hold your business hand is a must to building a successful business. Jules' support is invaluable and she continues to help Heartizan grow with her practical sales approach and the Live It, Love It, Sell It Methodology.

Grow your networks and start connecting, continue to share your stories and go live! Heartizan encourages this in one of our Facebook groups, The Crafters Display and we run monthly challenges. The majority of business owners hadn't livestreamed before and since completing our "Live for Five" they noticed their confidence growing and their presence on social media increasing. Sharing your stories, hopes, dreams, products and demos starts your business growth and you learn you don't have to post constantly in Facebook groups.

A lot of creatives spend their time in the crafting groups where they share their products and join in networking ladders, which I now know isn't really networking at all. Creatives appear to be obsessed with building their reaches, likers, followers and using their time ineffectively. I worked this out fairly quickly and I knew that the numbers meant absolutely nothing. Getting sales to me was a lot more important than dropping links in the crafting communities, doing like for likes and commenting on each other's page. These do have a place in the crafting world, however there is a lot more to building your brand and making sales. To start with, the crafting community is not our target audience and so I started there. I really looked into my clients' avatars and what their reason was to buy my products and with the knowledge and tools that Robin had given me, I grew my brand. I built up my connections and started going to offline networking events and met real people. I surprised myself with how confident I felt and how much passion shone through when I spoke about my businesses to other entrepreneurs. I even managed to stand up in front of some and speak publicly, though this really was pushing myself out of my comfort zone. Going live on Facebook or any of the other social media platforms came naturally to me and I knew "people buy from people." They were interested in my story and they related to me and my family. My children would also go live with me and even now they like to be part of my business. I had lots of plans to grow Cuddle Beds and create an ultimate all singing and all dancing multi-sensory product. This was even on the BBC but funding to get it from prototype to being manufactured was certainly an issue. I looked into grants and funding but I did not have the time to fully explore this option.

I moved out of the pet shop and I rented my first little unit in a beautiful business park. That was definitely one of my highs; I felt this was the time to really grow Cuddle Beds and to start selling them wholesale. I knew where I wanted my beds to be available in the high street and I contacted a few large retail stores. There was one in particular whose head buyer was interested in sleep and even spoke about it during events she attended, so I started to target her as a useful contact.

I sent the company information but I only got as far as the junior buyers and they did not think my products would be the right fit for their stores. I started a list of where I would like to sell, where I could be featured in magazines, radio and TV programmes. I was successful at getting my story out there and each time I had a good increase in sales. I even got paid by two magazines and my story continued to reach people. I knew exactly where my business was going and I had my plans and goals set out.

Unfortunately, things don't always turn out the way you want them to. A couple of close business friends advised me that running two businesses would be too difficult and there was just not enough time in the day, I thought I could do it to start with but it was just impossible. So I found a team of seamstresses to help with the sewing side of the business and the rest I fitted in around Heartizan, which was not easy as it started to consume me and take over my whole life, but I absolutely loved it.

Heartizan offers something no other marketplace does; it offers support, one to one contact, help and advice, business plans, toolkits, training, guest speakers and so much more! The team behind the marketplace are a fantastic group of creative people with so much skill and knowledge, which makes Heartizan truly amazing. My team had key people in their lives that have inspired them and kept them going through the struggles and challenges of life. We regularly run challenges within our groups and during Inspirational Women's Week we all wrote about those women in our lives. Here are some of their stories:

AMY'S STORY - RAINBOW POOCHY

My mum inspires and helps me through each day she is an amazing woman. She was given six months to live when she was born, and she has had arthritis since she was six years old. She never gave up, she kept fighting and became a chef. She lost her dad when she was twenty and then met my dad and had my brother. They fostered for eight years then adopted my sister and another brother. My Dad's parents and my

Mum's got ill, and my Mum looked after both sets of parents while finding out she was six months pregnant with me. Mum's mum moved in with us, Dad lost his mum, but mum continued to work and look after the family. Her mum became blind and had Alzheimer's, but she kept going. After all parents died, she took over the over 50s club that Nan founded, and she retired. She then got bored and set up her own catering business. She is now 70 years old and is still running a business taking care of Dad and helping hubby with me and my little one. She continues to help push me forward every day and still runs her club and a monthly bingo for charity. She is truly amazing, and I am so lucky; if I can be half the woman that she is, then I will be amazing too.

SUE'S STORY – EARTHGEMS

My big sister is amazing. She has been a Rheumatoid Arthritis warrior for all her adult life. She has had nearly all her joints either fused, resurfaced or replaced (only her hips are hers!). Yet despite all the pain she is often in, she still makes herself live as full and active life as she can have, even though we're now in our 60s. She's been a great support to our jewellery venture over the past five years or more, including funding our first kiln, commissioning pieces, helping at fairs, constantly sharing our items on social media and now helping with our Heartizan Shop listings. We think she's wonderful and we love her to bits!

VICKI'S STORY – CREATIONS – WHERE IDEAS COME ALIVE

At the age of 55, my mum was deeply into her crafts, having enrolled on floristry and cake decorating courses, learning about sugar craft and was really excited. Then she was diagnosed with what we hoped was carpel tunnel but was in fact Parkinson's Disease. It was a complete shock for us all, but my mum has from then until now, some 10 years later, never let it stop her from doing what she enjoys. She turns her hand to all kinds of crafts, baking, cake decorating, card making, knitting, crochet, random projects she has seen on Facebook.

You name it, she will try it, sometimes to our amusement. I still laugh at the rather large snowman she made out of plastic cups! It was like an episode of Blue Peter! She is strong and will do anything for us girls. My mum is my inspiration!

Secondly, there is my youngest sister. As a family, we were all very excited about the new identical twin boys who were about to come into the world. My own daughter, my first child, had been born five months before. I still remember the call I had from my mum whilst I was on my way to work that April. She told me my sister had gone into labour. She was early, not due for another month. I assured my mum it would be okay, to be told but it's not okay, she lost one of the babies. I lost a nephew that day, but my sister lost her son. We were all devastated, shocked, but we got through it and my sister was so brave. I can't begin to imagine how she felt that day losing a child. Adam is never forgotten and is spoken about often. His twin turned 16 this April and he also has a 13 year old younger brother. They are wonderful lads, hard-working and kind. My youngest sister is my inspiration!

Finally, there is my middle sister. She was the first to have a baby – he is now 17 and is taller than me by far. He has faced struggles, found it hard to make friends and has dyslexia. Despite his struggles, he passed his exams, enough to get him onto his Art course at College. He is the most wonderful young man and dotes on his younger siblings. Then there is my niece who was diagnosed with Asperger's and again struggles with day-to-day emotions and feelings. She has good days, bad days and very bad days. Then there is my youngest nephew who has autism, attends a special needs school and is classed as non-verbal, although every day he finds new ways to communicate, whether that is using Makaton signing or chattering away and communicating with us in his own ways. He loves to sing and knows all the words to all the songs in The Greatest Showman. This is Me reduces us to tears! These kids are achieving so much because of one person, their mum, my sister, who's also my inspiration.

So, it is no wonder that with these three inspirational women by my side, that when I had cause to be strong and leave a 17-year relation-ship when it turned mentally and emotionally abusive, I knew I could do it! I am now a single mum, with two gorgeous kids, working full time and running a business.

DI'S STORY – BEE BELLE KEEPSAKES

I've always loved sewing. I can remember making my own dolls clothes sewing them by hand from about the age of 11. I took up sewing at school, using a machine for the first time and made my first outfit. From then on I made clothes for myself and skirts for my mum, soft furnishings and even went on to make my brothers suit and my flowers girls dress for my first wedding.

Back then this was only a past time of mine as I had attended college for my NNEB and then became a nanny. I always wanted to be a stay at home mum as I loved children and wanted to be there for mine all the time and luckily I was in a position to be able to do that.

After having my first 2 children and when my youngest was about 6, I decided to become a registered childminder. This would still allow me to be at home with my children while keeping my hand in with work. I did this until I became pregnant with my 3rd child. Years passed and my children grew up and my eldest daughter had our first grandchild. She wanted to go back to work so I started to look after my granddaughter.

Fast forward to 2 years later and I wanted to start to earn a little money for myself so with thinking cap on, it was either go back out to work and not have a clue what to do or do what I love and start my own business. The more I thought about it the more the latter sounded better and better and with the support of my new partner, decided to go ahead.

The name came to me in an instant which was my granddaughters pronunciation of her own name which was Bee Belle.....translated as Isabelle.

My theory was that I would make children's clothing so with that in mind I order a few patterns and started to make some samples. I made a few dresses and pinafores and made some dungarees and popped them on my page that I created on Facebook……and waited….and waited…..and waited. Being so naïve and not knowing anything about marketing I just presumed people would see these and swarm like flies to buy my items. After seeing other businesses online and popping out orders left right and centre I wondered what I was doing wrong.

After a few weeks a friend of mine contacted me and asked if I would be able to make some oven gloves and an apron for her grandson. I made my own easy pattern and that was my first order. I'd thought about making toys but knew about the CE testing and decided not to go down that route but made a few bunnies for my grand daughter and grandson and my cousins' children. It was then at this point that someone contacted me and asked if it would be possible to make 12 bears out of her dads shirts as he had recently passed away….wow, 12 I thought. This actually ended up as 16 as more of her family wanted them.

I decided then that selling children's clothes wasn't an option. I couldn't compete with the prices of the high street shop and supermarkets. The memory bears that I had made went down like a storm so made the decision to take my business in a whole new direction.

I now make memory keepsake cushions, bears, rabbits, in fact any animal you can think of. I've just started creating keepsake keyrings, the idea of which came from one of my recent customers.

I've always suffered from Migraines and Vertigo but just over 3 years ago, I suffered from the most debilitating episode of Vertigo that I've ever experienced. I couldn't move as every single movement made my head spin, even sitting still didn't help and the pain in my head was unbearable. The pain I was experiencing was on a whole new level. I thought I had something seriously wrong with me. This lasted for months, the pain eventually subsided along with the vertigo but it would come back every few weeks. The doctor said it was nothing but eventually sent me to the hospital as I had constant noise in my ears which would make the headaches worse. The hospital tests concluded that I was having vestibular migraines. I was given an exercise to do which helped immensely every time I had an attack.

This has eventually dwindled and I only experience it once in a while now but it can come on at any time, there is nothing specific that triggers it all and when I do get an attack, I hate noise as I find it difficult to even listen to people on the phone as it hurts my head. Mobile phone screens are now a no no, especially scrolling as it brings on the vertigo.

Even though I've never classed this an illness, it's something I've learnt to live with and can now manage it better with the exercises when I do get an attack.

I'm thankful that I am at home most days because of this which allows me to spend time with my grandchildren and family plus working full time on my business means I can dedicate more time to helping it to grow.

MANDY-JAYNE'S STORY - LUCY LOCKETS STUDIO

I live on a farm in Cornwall UK with my husband Charlie and my Great Dane Narnia Bug and this my dream.

My handmade journey started in 1993. My mom and I owned a small collectors and antique shop, we used to often buy job lots of jewellery and get broken bits and bobs, I started off by just repairing the items to put in the shop. Some was quite old fashioned and some sadly beyond repair so I started to design and repurpose the broken bits. These sold really well in the shop and by the following year, I started buy beads and findings to make my own range of reproduction antique jewellery.

I did this for many years, I loved giving back something its life and allowing it to be loved and used for many years to come! I guess I actually felt sorry for it! At the same time I attended fairs and shows and won a couple of awards for my designs. Fast forward a few years and my dad was diagnosed with prostrate cancer and it was terminal which was a real shock! We'd recently moved house and taken on a new shop, sadly we had to close the shop to look after dad, it was such a hard and terrible time in my life.

Mom and I moved house again and mom started to lose her sight in one eye but despite that, we started 'up selling' collectables online but she wasn't well at all. She had been diagnosed with breast cancer a few years ago but then she had a new diagnosis of breast cancer.

Her appendix ruptured and she had sepsis too, she then admitted she was finding it harder to help with the business.

I had always loved photography, my grandad had loved it and had taught me a lot and my uncle was a photographer in his spare time, entering and winning many competitions. I already had a good camera for taking product images for our eBay and website so I started offering my photography services to people, this was before the camera phone had really taken off and I was well in demand. I did holiday home portfolios, product photography and animals mainly, that went on for a couple of years. I attended various courses and loved my work but mom had started to slow down and when I asked her if she was ok she said she had a pain in her chest. She finally went to see the doctors, 12 weeks on and she had the devastating news that she had pancreatic cancer. She was to face a massive 12 hour operation, well mom was always strong and she sailed through the operation and was out of the hospital a few days later. She did amazing and our Doctor called her Mrs Miracle, but things soon changed and 6 months later she passed away very suddenly from a delayed complication. I was devastated, shortly after with no place to go so I moved in with my fiancé and for months I did nothing at all. I just sat or walked my Great Dane Lucy Locket, she'd been by my side with dad and mom and had always got me through!

Then on the morning of Halloween 2014, I decided to do something, mom wouldn't have wanted me to just give up, she always believed in me and my creative side. She was creative too, having attended Birmingham school of Art. She'd left me some money to start up on my own again doing something. I didn't want to go back to the photography as mom had always helped me but jewellery was something that I enjoyed and I found therapeutic to do! So that was that I started to make jewellery again, I'd soon got a shoe box full and I had my first order a couple of weeks of launching. I traded under the name of Akamar Balla Jewellery as that was the kennel club name of my previous and first Great Dane.

I did that for a couple of years and then I decided in 2016 to buy a vinyl cutter and heat press to press my own bags for my jewellery, that was like a giant business snowball! From there, I bought a sublimation printer then a mug press and I started making general gifts. Life was getting better, I got married and Lucy Locket my Great Dane was my bridesmaid!

Then life took another horrible turn, this time my beloved Lucy Locket had a lump on her toe, we took her to the vet who advised to her age 10 years old just keep an eye on it. Though he still needed to check her over and with a worried look on his face, he felt her tummy and ordered an ultrasound scan to be carried out. He then informed me that he was worried and that something wasn't right, a few tests later we found that she had a large growth. After an exploratory op we were told the growth was too big to be removed, it was a large and on her kidney, likely to be cancer. We were told she would only have a few weeks.

That was November and she made it to Christmas but then she started to get worse and I lost my Lucy Locket on the 21st of January 2017. I'd always had a dog in my life and I felt my life had ended along with hers! I'd lost my companion and my best friend. I started to fall into depression fast and I knew I needed to pull myself out of it and quick! I asked Lucy to send me another dog, a lot like her but not exactly so! Days later and by chance I spotted a Great Dane pup just like my Lucy and I knew that I had to have this pup. A couple of days later she was *on her way home with us and I believe she was sent by Lucy for me to love.*

I started to make things for Narnia, she attended puppy class so I first made a treat and poop bag, then we started to make show accessories, collars, leads and a T-shirt for me with her name on it! Then people started to ask me where I got it all from and I began to get orders, so I decided to set up a business once again. I did really well attending dog shows and selling online when I could, though we only had a basic broadband and it was a real struggle. The other problem was the rain, if it poured down at a dog show, we had to rush to get things packed away but then an idea sprung into my head, what if I bought an old caravan and converted it to a shop? I was quite surprised when the day after I spotted a scrap dealer selling off an old caravan for £50, it was a mess inside and damp but the chassis was good! So I bought it and the work to convert into a shop started. My husband Charlie converted it all using upcycled wood for the inside.

In May 2018 I opened the Crazy Dog Pawtique, a gift shop specialising in animal themed gifts for pets and people. I became myself again and I started to make new friends, I also I became a Parish Councillor and was elected as the local Climate Change coordinator. I had always been interested in what my dad called 'saving stuff '. I started to make more of a wider range of gifts again, really coming full circle and yet growing as I did and discovering myself or should I say rediscovering! I renamed the business to mark this new start and in honour of Lucy Locket, I named my business Lucy Locket's Studio. I then started to fuse glass as a hobby, another thing which can be recycled and that was Christmas 2018. By very early 2019 I'd added my glass pieces to my very wide range of handmade gifts and jewellery. We then got a 'fibre' to our premises, 300mbps which allowed me to sell properly online. That was amazing, after years of driving to the local fast food place to use the connection just to upload my photos.

I then did something else that I feel has rocketed me to success and that was joining The Heartizan Marketplace, 1st as a seller and then as a

Madmin. Heartizan, for me has actually been life changing, Chrissie and the team are so supportive and amazing.

Heartizan have given me the knowledge and the skill to promote me and my business on social media and to have confidence in what I do, I love being part of this amazing marketplace. I now feel that I can grow,

I plan to open a teaching workshop in 2020 where I will be teaching, running workshops and sharing my skills with those who want to learn to craft for fun or a business. I will offer talks on upcycling for craft and profit, something I am so excited about, so watch this space!

BERNIE'S STORY – UNIQUE HANDCRAFTED CHIC

My own daughters inspire me every day. I am very lucky to have two beautiful girls. And they have both faced many challenges in their young lives. My eldest daughter has overcome so many life challenges and strives and pushes hard every single day to achieve her goals through her two online businesses and is achieving some small but fantastic results. My youngest is just crazy and no matter what she is faced with she always manages to put a smile on everyone's face.

They both have both been such a support to me through my illness and through their dad's recent illness. They make me very proud to be their mum. They both inspire me and always make me smile and I love them very much.

They both have both been such a support to me through my illness and through their dad's recent illness. They make me very proud to be their mum. They both inspire me and always make me smile and I love them very much.

EMMA'S STORY – EM'S PAPERLOVE

My daughter is my inspiration, she keeps me going. I think my illnesses are just as hard for her as they are for me. She used to have a mum who could do everything with her and now she has a mum who she has to check something won't hurt me before she asks if we can do something. As a 12-year-old, she shouldn't have to do that. I am very lucky to have her.

MY STORY – CHRISSIE – THE CUDDLE BED COMPANY AND HEARTIZAN

At the age of 30, I was pregnant with my second daughter and I ran a specialist unit for adults with autism. At the time I loved my job, but it was incredibly stressful and challenging. I was a home leader of four adults who could not be with their families because of where they were on the spectrum. I was my team's Internal Verifier for NVQ qualifications, and I used to have regular meetings with the External Verifier. During one of these meetings, she told me that I was wasted there and that I should go to university and train as a mental health nurse.

At the time, I did not agree. However, the more I thought about it, the more university and retraining appealed to me. I had my beautiful daughter a few weeks early after lots of complications and I fell into depression, I had Borderline Post-Natal Depression. I couldn't sleep, I didn't want anyone to touch her, I cleaned the house obsessively and it was a very difficult time for us. I also lived with an alcoholic partner who was cheating on me with his ex-wife which I found out when I was seven months pregnant.

I decided life had to be better than this, I had my fair share of bad luck, bad relationships and hard life lessons from an early age. Life was surely more! That conversation with the Verifier kept popping back into my head and so I decided to apply for university. I did not go back to work and when my daughter was six months old; instead, I started my university course in Birmingham. I live in beautiful Gloucestershire and commuting there every day was quite a challenge in itself.

I graduated with honours and recommendations from the principle and my life changed for the better. I still had challenges and hardships to face in the future, but I was truly happy.

Since becoming a creative, I have met so many inspirational women and I am so very proud to have brought together a team that we call our Heartizan family. They are incredible people; we have an amazing male Madmin and over 35 women and the team is growing all the time. I continue to be inspired by my team; they drive me along with my own goals and my plans for the future.

HEARTIZAN - HOW TO SHOW UP CONSISTENTLY

AN INTERVIEW WITH DOMINIC DE SOUZA – FOUNDER OF DREAM AGAIN MARKETING

Dominic is an expert in story-telling, he was a guest speaker in one of our Facebook Groups and this is some of his interview:

"That's why I say if you want to be interesting you need to be interested in them first. This is what an adult does to a child, you express interest in them first and then that elicits them then to respond and grow. It's like you walk into a party or you walk into a bar; don't expect people to be interested in you. They will be after you've expressed interest in them; ask them all kinds of questions about what they're doing and so on. Same thing with your business and your marketing."

"You've got your story, why you're doing things, who you are and how it relates to what you're doing, and then you spend most of your time not just telling people, here's how amazing all of my things are and all my services are going to do this. But then spend more of your time celebrating the people who love you. Talk about them, talk about what they're doing, talk about who they are and what they were going through and how hard life can be.

"So instead of just being a service business or a product-making business, you are now a story-making business and you are providing products to sort of cement or to create artefacts of these stories."

- Surround yourself with like-minded people.
- Make peace with the past.
- Invest in coaches, programmes, technical support and training.
- Join Facebook groups.
- Read books.
- Write blogs.
- Follow creative bloggers.
- Collaborate.
- Remember where you came from and how it all started.
- Feel the fear and do it anyway.
- Practice your mind set.
- Do random acts of kindness.
- Be grateful.
- I believe the universe will help and we just need to believe. Start a journal and write things down, your plans, your why and your dreams.
- Have a vision board in your home, crafting space or at work.
- Take time out and for yourself.
- Follow Ed Troxell Creative – "show up, deliver and engage".

PRO-CRAFT-INATING

I admit it, I pro-craft-inate all the time. I get lost in the black hole of Facebook and Pinterest or I keep myself busy with doing absolutely nothing. Like most people I have my Debbie Downer days where I can't find my motivation and it becomes lost under the mountain of admin. Overwhelm can sneak up and kick you in the butt at any time and just when you least expect it. Juggling kids, home, business, furry friends, friends, work, admin, life struggles, challenges and fun times is a lot to fit in to your life.

You are allowed time out; procrastination is good for you and allows time for your brain to rest. However, you need more productive days and procrastination needs to be monitored and only allowed out of the craft room once in a while.

I learnt the biggest lessons during this time, and I am sure I made lots of mistakes too, but I kept going. I connected with a lot of amazing people, other business owners, coaches, experts and I made a lot of connections as well as a few enemies too! I honestly do not know why some people feel the need to try and destroy your dreams or to make life extremely hard for other people.

I must admit I will never find it easy and I am constantly learning but I needed help as I knew Heartizan could not grow and I could not do it all myself. My trust was tested on many occasions and for the majority of the time, I have no idea why. My Madmin team are now strong and they have the same vision as me, I am extremely grateful to all of them. Heartizan is just not about my story, it is the story of many.

Before we built this solid foundation, we needed a selling platform, creatives, a plan, some amazing content and a team of support to really become a unique and magical marketplace. The name of Heartizan was the easy part but the next year was hard and Cuddle Beds took many hits in favour of Heartizan. I kind of juggled them both but it was impossible to build a new business and continue to grow another.

The next step was to launch the marketplace and with the help of Jules White (sales coach) Eleanor Goold (copy writer) and Ed Troxell (The Hey Ed membership group) and I was ready to take Heartizan forward. We decided to beta test for three months and see how well the marketplace performed. I spent my days and long nights teaching myself how to edit, publish, list and know all about SEO so I could help the creatives who joined us. My knowledge base grew and as a team we built the business, so it was ready to go outside of the Heartizan groups.

We had good and bad feedback, but I was very proud of what we had built, a fabulous customer experience and sharing knowledge to the crafting community definitely lit us all up. We knew we weren't as big as Etsy or Not on the High Street and we were told that these kinds of sales platforms were overly saturated, but we knew Heartizan was special and would help a lot of crafters. There was no other marketplace that was built by crafters for crafters. Eleanor Goold wrote our sales pitch and she came up with the three packages that are our subscriptions to the Marketplace.

THE CRAFTERS DISPLAY

This is a great package for start-up business or when you just need a magical marketplace to sell your handcrafted products on. There is no invoices to send and your accounts will be a dream. You just have to give your customers the link to your fabulous products or direct them to the marketplace. Heartizan will share your products on all of the major social media platforms, write about you in our newsletter and of course go live on our main page.

THE ARTISAN TOOLBOX

This package is for creatives who are ready to learn, streamline and upscale their businesses. Members will learn more about social media, how to promote and market your business and you will increase your knowledge base. Members can do this by having access to learning materials and guest speakers along with a very supportive group.

THE IMAGINARIUM

This is where the magic happens, as this package is for the creatives who are serious about their businesses and want to take them up to the next level. Creative business owners have access to mentorship and a programme that will make their businesses ready for success!

A couple of months after the launch, I was lucky enough to win a stand at the Autumn Fair. I had been selected by Theo Paphitis and I had very little time to prepare but this was an incredible and exciting opportunity which I grabbed with both hands.

In our amazing Small Business Sunday group, we were all invited to apply to win a stand at the Autumn Fair. Theo selected a short list of thirty-six SBS winners which was announced on Twitter and through the Autumn Fair. After what seemed like forever, the lucky twelve were announced and I was incredibly fortunate to be one of those twelve. The fair is an incredible experience and it is where businesses sell to wholesalers. The press is there, and Autumn Fair team make sure your business gets good exposure and are very supportive.

We then had just six weeks to prepare and organise our stands and fellow winner Nikki Hollier from the fabulous business Border in a Box was my absolute rock! We had met at the SBS event in February and have stayed in touch, there was a considerable amount of work to get done in preparation for the fair and having her sound advice and knowledge got me through those chaotic six weeks! We remain in touch and I am grateful that I have made such good business friends through SBS.

I was also assigned a brilliant Autumn Fair Manager, Gareth Watkins, who talked me through the process several times and even visited me during the fair. Without his calming influence and sound advice, along with all the logistics, I don't think I would have been ready or prepared for the big day.

My daughter Mollie also helped me so much, not only on "build up and break down days" of my stand but with all the design work too. On the day before he doors opened, we entered the fair to set up and found the SBS pavilion situated in the Lighting section. The stands surrounding us were so very impressive and I must admit I had quite a wobble right there and then, thinking that ours was just not good enough. Theo's opening words for the Small Business Sunday event back in February resonated in my head," shut the **** up!" This statement related to small businesses thinking small and that we can't keep up with the big boys. So, I pulled up my big girl pants and my daughter and I made it work; we ended up feeling very proud of my stand and were ready to get selling to wholesalers. On the very first day, buyers visited my stand telling me it looked amazing and it drew them in and from then on I really found my feet. Both Mollie and I loved our first day. Sharing it with our fellow winners on the pavilion was amazing; we all quickly formed relationships and supported each other.

It was such an incredible experience and it totally changed my outlook of my business, my confidence and what I could achieve. I spoke to other stand-holders who gave me some excellent advice along with everyone who visited my stand, whether they were the press, the SBS Crew, the Autumn Fair team or traders. I have never felt so supported and valued as a small business owner as I did at the fair and I would like to thank everyone who visited me. This includes Gareth, Rob; **the Key Account Director**, Jules White; sales coach from **Live It, Love it, Sell it,** Vicki Smith, a Madmin from **Heartizan,** followers of my page who visited my stand to introduce themselves to me, Lloyd from Robert Dyas and of course the man himself, Theo!

The rest of the week was just as incredible. There were fabulous guest speakers from Not on the High Street and John Lewis, but the most exciting day had to be Theo's visit! He visited each and every winner; he really listened to us, allowed us many photo opportunities and showed just how much he supported us.

On the third day, my twins came to demonstrate my products on my stand. Theo visited, and they were so excited to meet him! All my children know about Theo, Dragons' Den and Small Business Sunday. They had their photo taken with him and were filmed too; they certainly had an amazing day! I started to feel like a good role model again and I knew they were proud of their mum.

The next couple of months was the run up to Christmas, which was amazing for Heartizan. We had a huge amount of sales and our brand was starting to get out there. I was busy with Cuddle Beds as it is the busiest time of year for me too and I worked up until Christmas Eve. As always, I ended up in bed, but I carried on learning and expanding on what I already knew.

The first few months were quite a struggle; we took a lot of knocks in the crafting community groups, though I really do not know why.

Madmins left for various reasons and our morale took a huge dive. My health deteriorated again, and I was in more pain than I had ever been in before. I could not sit at my table or my desk for very long and my back felt like it was broken. I could not spend much time working and I slipped into depression. My team rallied round and somehow, we got through.

The Small Business Sunday event rolled around again, and I took my daughter with me which helped me pull myself out of the dark and back into my normal positive self. It was another inspirational event and we got to see the filming from The Autumn Fair. Theo had amazing guest speakers and we met up with the Robert Dyas team again. I was introduced to their PR lady who wanted to write a feature about Cuddle Beds. This featured on several online publications and I also had an article published in *The Lady magazine*.

The following month I had an appointment with a rheumatologist, and he informed me that I had some spinal problems and maybe osteoporosis. I had more tests and scans and was put on another course of medication, which made me even worse. Fortunately, I did not have osteoporosis, but I did have two degenerative spinal issues which meant two more diagnoses. During times like these, it is hard to remain focussed, but I had a crowdfunding campaign to launch and we had invested in a stand at the Handmade Festival in London. This is hosted by Kirstie Allsopp who will be signing the first copy of this very book. Exciting times were ahead, and we needed to restructure our team to continue with our goals.

Creating our Heartizan community has been one of the best experiences; we offer so much support and we gain so much wonderful feedback, some of which are captured below.

"Oh my goodness, I just had my first "Zoom" chat with Chrissie Lowery, after being so nervous as to whether I would be able to technically achieve it! I did it and was so please with myself for overcoming my fear of an actual life chat. I did have a hiccup towards the end with the Sky falling off though. What a lovely and inspiring lady Chrissie is

– she is totally amazing with what she has achieved with her business in such a relatively short space of time. If I can achieve just a teeny tiny weeny bit of what Chrissie has, I will be more than happy. I've only been with Heartizan for two weeks and so far I have learnt so much. Thank you everyone, it is an amazing group to be part of". – Susan Simms, founder of Button Buddies.

I would like to compliment the entire Heartizan Madmin for their support, encouragement and all-round helpfulness with the groups that I have been shown over the 2 weeks since joining and opening my shop, even though I have not needed much at all. I would most specially to say a huge thank you to my personal Madmin Dale Patrick-Evans as he has helped me out so much and published my listing at times when I would not expect it, such as very late at night.

So, thank you for all being such a friendly and welcoming bunch of people" – A Heartizan Creative

"Chrissie you are such an inspiration and what I love is that you share all that knowledge with all of us so that we can (and do) grow our own businesses. I love being part of your Madmin Team and we are all happy to support you in this amazing opportunity for small businesses. Vicki Smith founder of Creations – Where Ideas Come Alive

"Look who won a Meet the Maker spot on the Heartizan website last week for participating in a Live for Five video challenge in the exclusive marketplace group? Little ol' me. So, flipping grateful and happy about this" – Davina Kecun founder of IndigoSky2Knit

"The help and support you get is the best I have ever seen and received. An amazing team, best thing I ever did for my business was to join. I am forever grateful, and I want to shout you all from the rooftops of how proud I am to be part of this crafty family" - Amy Searle founder of Rainbow Poochy

Pro-craft-inating or procrastination is something we all do and maybe the true meaning of the word in the non-crafting sense is all about standing back and assessing your situation but not actually getting a lot of your tasks completed. In creative terms, I believe it is all about crafting when things get bad or sad, I know crafting takes me out of my own head and allows me time to heal. Crafting is more than a hobby, a business, a new skill, it is a happy place where nothing but craft and dreams are allowed. We can get stuck in the black hole of social media or we just can't finish the new products that we have started and we can't get our crafting mojo back.

This is where your tribe, you crew, you crafting friends or your business family can kick you back into gear, with love of course!

HEARTIZAN - HOW TO KEEP MOVING FORWARD

- Get an accountability buddy.
- Set achievable goals and targets.
- Journal your thoughts and feelings.
- Take time out when you need to – you can't pour from an empty cup!
- Save your reviews and put them into an album or a blog.
- Look back at how far you have come and reward yourself for you small and big wins.
- Hire a coach or join The Imaginarium Facebook membership group (which is amazing value for money).
- Keep positive and rely on your gut (this has never let me down).
- Ask your followers advice and let them guide you in relation to your products.
- Set up a Mailchimp account or similar (Mailchimp is free for the first 2000 contacts).
- Link your social media accounts and schedule in advance.
- Track your sales and market to your target audience.
- Use forms like Survey Monkey which can also be linked to Mailchimp.

- Try selling in a smarter way.
- Follow Joelle Byrne who can help you gain passive income for creative businesses.
- Work on your touch points and ensure each one has a call to action where the customer can buy your products.
- Set up the shop feature on your Facebook page and Instagram and link it to your website or a selling platform.
- Engage your audience and keep them updated with your business journey as well as your products
- Reply to all of your comments on social media; this helps you get seen on the Facebook algorithms.
- If you go live, ensure you have good content that is relevant to your audience and your business. Have a call to action and try to go live for at least twenty minutes on Facebook.
- Set up your own group and link it to your page; Facebook is all about community and as Ed Troxell often says, "the party is in the comments". Your group could be very different to your business and could be more about helping others.
- Use your personal profile in a business way, not by sharing all of your products there but you can add your links to the "about section" and add nine featured photos which should be about your business and your products.
- Utilise the social media platforms that have stories and add text with your price, website, selling platform or other call to action information.
- Test, test and test again.

JOELLE BYRNE – CREATIVE CASH – AN INTERVIEW ABOUT EBOOKS

"The whole point of it was to try and make it a step by step plan that wasn't too overwhelming, but gave a real solid advice to take you from A to Z if you are now feeling a bit frazzled, maybe not having enough time to create more in orders to make more money, but feeling as though you want to create more money in your business. And that's where the book is coming from. That's where it's positioned, and it's

directed exactly at craft as creators, artists and people who make gorgeous items. The whole point is basically to take you from falling a little bit short of time, short of patience and thinking, "Oh, do I even want to carry on with this?" to a point where you feel as though you're able to make additional income streams in your business and to make passive income and to really build it from the foundations up. So, it's just a 10-step plan with loads of techniques and information that will hopefully get their creative juices flowing to get people to come up with ideas of how they could generate more cash in their business."

"So actually, streamlining the idea and the thought process is the most difficult bit of writing and releasing an eBook and the technology side of it isn't that hard. You can literally create an eBook in a Word document, and you can create your cover on Picmonkey or Canva. Those who have got access to Photoshop, connect your cover images and be as straightforward as that and then save it as a PDF document. And so you get all your ideas down on paper and go from there."

"You can repurpose content from your blog to try and build some interest around the topic and run some competitions. There's lots of ways to market an eBook, and you could make it downloadable as well. It's something you are probably already doing, and then the potential is pretty big."

"The latest eBook that I've just released is 60 pages in total. The thing is if you've got a specific message, you don't want to be going over the top because when you write an eBook, it can become a little bit monotonous. If your message is still unique to your business then anything from 50 pages onwards, as long as it gets the message across and isn't too brief. I wouldn't recommend advertising something as an eBook that is only 10 pages long because it's more of a guide or an introduction and it needs to be something that you would consider to be a book. But you also need to remember that eBooks are not an ordinary book either and they are smaller, but the content is always going to be less spread out. It is a little bit more condensed and putting images and things in there as well makes it more appealing".

SAMANTHA HAWKINS – NLP PRACTITIONER AND EMPOWERMENT COACH – HOW TO KEEP POSITIVE

"I'm sure that nothing I say is going to be particularly new, but I always find that it's nice to have reminders. So, I have a list of 10 top tips to help you feel positive and calm but sometimes external factors and the best will in the world, it can really be hard sometimes. Then you just need that little reminder just to think, yeah, everything is happening. And even on a day where there's hardly anything to feel positive about, if you're feeling really ill or really down or the kids are playing off or whatever, there's always something, even if it's just the sun shining. So, my first tip is to remember to focus on what you want rather than what you don't want. So, you're filtering for positive, so I'll give you an example of that. Look around your room and count all the things that are black. Now tell me how many yellow things there are but without looking around the room. That is more difficult as you were just filtering for black things and, without looking, the yellow is harder to recall. So, it's the same with positivity and negativity. If we are negative or we focus on all the things that we've got going on and all the things are going wrong that is all we will see. However, if you filter for positive even though you still have all those things going on, it will help you to become more positive and to focus on those things rather than anything going wrong in your life."

"So, another thing is to learn is to put yourself first sometimes and to feel okay about that.

This is a big thing I still struggle with especially when you're a mother as well or a father, but I do think it's harder for mothers. People with chronic illness who are generally high achievers and are usually perfectionists and they are used to putting everyone first even when they feel really ill."

"Learning to meditate is also a way to help keep positive and is my way of being able to breathe. I've learnt how to come out of my head

and into my body now and I have different ways of being able to get out of my overthinking head and just relax."

"I know art and music are my two things to help with positivity and I can do them and completely lose myself in them and that's my distraction. And that is my equivalent of someone just sitting on the sofa doing nothing. I have to be doing something, but it's getting out of my head and into my body. It can be a hard one, but I'm trying not to feel guilty for doing something for myself. You can also make time to be with your kids and to have, even if you know you're working, you could put aside 20 minutes playing a game with them and have some fun."

"I also do daily affirmations and I really believe that they help us stay positive because you're looking yourself in the eyes, which is really hard to start with and you say it three times out loud, ideally three times a day to start with."

SHARING THE LOVE

Heartizan is made up of fabulous creatives who support and help each other, whether they are part of the team or they are in our groups or they sell on our magical marketplace. We share our journey, our stories, our good times, our bad times and above all we help each other grow.

This is Heartizan's ethos, to help and support others and to really connect with our fellow creatives, as after all we are working for the same reason, to sell our products. I have found in some creative groups that people do not like to share or let others know how they have achieved or learnt something but when you do this together, it becomes a whole lot better. Collaboration is definitely the key to growth; helping each other and reaching out will do wonders for your businesses.

On our Heartizan page and groups we like to make our creatives visible and confident and now the Madmin team are passing on our core values to everyone who joins us or just hangs out in our public groups. The number of us who have now got awards, can confidently go live, pitch to complete strangers or reach out to each other is amazing and is growing all the time. By helping each other and rising up we can certainly do amazing things. We encourage our creatives to blog and then we post them on our website too; this excerpt is from a super creative who is part of The Imaginarium.

Sue Frecklington is the most selfless creative I know (and most of us are pretty giving and caring) and she has a non-profit business to raise money for finding a cure for AHC (Alternating Hemiplegia of Childhood). She owns the wonderful business Granny Maud and the Old Grump and she makes the most amazing quilts and soft furnishings.

Here is her story:

"Many years ago, in the second world war, my Dad was stationed in Iceland. He was one of a group of soldiers lost in a snowstorm in Iceland. He was rescued by an Icelandic family and they became firm friends. Sometime after he returned home, I was born, and in my teens began a pen friendship with Gunny, a girl of similar age in the family. It is Gunny's granddaughter Sunna, who has AHC for which there is as yet no cure. Sunna is amazingly happy but her condition is extremely debilitating. She has terrible episodes almost every day, – sometimes life-threatening episodes."

"Serious quilting was supposed to be a hobby for my retirement, but having supplied the family, I then had to look for another reason to sew. About the same time, we became aware of Sunna's rare illness. For two years I helped to raise funds to find a cure by doing a yearly sponsored cycle ride. The final year was the distance between Lincoln and Reykjavik – over 1700m, but I do not like asking the same people every year to sponsor me, so I went back to the sewing, selling what I could at craft fairs, and teaching, this time with my husband's help, as he enjoys making things with wood. He has also developed an interest in Steam Punk jewellery."

"Alternating Hemiplegia of Childhood, which is one of the most complex neurological disorders known to man, has a prevalence of

1/1.000.000. It incorporates many of the symptoms of other neurological diseases and has so many different elements and symptoms, always changing, that it is very difficult to explain to another person what goes on. One child with the illness may react in a different way to another. It can cause episodes of spasms, paralysis, seizures, and excruciating pain."

"In a way, I am paying back what they did for my family – after all without them I would not be here!"

GRANNY MAUD, WORKING TO FIND A CURE FOR AHC!

Our challenges are intended to push our creatives out of their comfort zones and the winners feature on our home page.

One of these challenges was to write some mini stories. As it was February, we chose love stories, and these had to part of our book.

HEARTIZAN LOVE STORIES

Our Heartizan love stories are compiled into a collection put together during a challenge in one of our groups, The Artisan Tool Box. During this challenge our amazing Artisans had to carry out a task each day for a week; this was to get us all thinking about love and Valentine's Day and how to promote your business.

My Heartizan love story is all about us! I am single so I don't really do anything on February 14th, however I will be celebrating my children, my friends and my Heartizan family. I called my team "Madmins" for a little bit of fun; we are all a happy crazy group with huge big hearts, and we love to support and help other crafters. Over the last few years we have built up an incredible team and we now have the strongest and most giving Madmins that we have ever had. I love each and every one and I am forever grateful for the support and faith that they have in me. My part of the Heartizan love stories collection is very humbling for me and even though I tell my Madmins how much they mean to me and how damn lucky I am to have them; words just cannot describe how thankful I am.

My family life is beginning to be almost back to 'normal' now; my children are over most of their difficult times and are all in supportive and wonderful schools which allows them to access their education without stress or conflict. My health is managed the best way it can be, and I have found that working on one business and then the other is the best way forward for me. My Cuddle Bed business is my baby and I will be launching a fantastic sensory range by the end of the year. Heartizan is now flying and I cannot wait to see it grow and mature. Next year will be amazing for both businesses; my three youngest children will be all in the same school and my other daughter will be in her second year at university studying graphic design. My eldest daughter is a manager in a large restaurant chain, and she juggles her work and home balance much better than her Mum! I am so very proud of all my children who are amazing human beings with the biggest hearts and beautiful souls.

JANE FROM MAY CONTAIN SPARKLE

"Hi everyone, I am Jane and I create gifts which make you smile through my business May Contain Sparkle."

"I have always loved colour and being creative in my own home. In fact, I come from a long line of creative people going back many generations. I personally like to give gifts which are unusual, with a little humour and if it is personalised all the better, so I started creating my own."

"I started my business in January 2017 as a distraction from being a carer. Being a carer for a family member was extremely hard and distressing which eventually made me poorly. The stress was just too much but making a gift for someone distracted me for a short time. I am no longer a carer but continued with my business as I just love it and I now have lovely repeat customers."

"I feel so lucky to be able to spend my time with gorgeous paint colours, pretty papers and ribbons. Of course, I claim not to have an addiction but between you and me I do. I just can't resist, and my "collection" has taken over my home as my husband will definitely agree with."

"I currently make plaques, signs, wreaths, frames and lots of other pretty items.

My best part of the day is receiving a review or message from a happy customer, I love it. I pride myself on good customer service as that is the way I would like to be treated.

I am new to Heartizan, but I have already been welcomed with open arms."

DAVINA FROM INDIGOSKY2KNIT

"I have one hell of a tale! I have always wanted to be a mum, for as long as I can remember, and I knew when that happened, I'd not want to be sacrificing time with my children while I went out to a job. I was 31 before I had my first baby, and in the meantime found some satisfaction in care work. A year after marrying my soul mate, we had our first baby. Life had thrown us a curve ball and he found himself out of work as I started maternity leave from the NHS."

"We then had a couple of years of struggle while he couldn't find work and I had another baby. After the 2nd baby was born, and following advice from friends, I launched Indigosky2Knit in 2012. At the same time hubby decided to quit looking for work in admin and launched his own graphic design business too. I'd been knitting since I was 7, when my eldest sister had her first baby. When I had my first baby, I started writing on a cloth nappy forum, and on there I came into contact with the WAHM (Work at Home Mum) world. Seeing that I could use my love for yarn crafts to create a business opened the door to a dream. Initially I didn't really think or want to make a lot of money from it, I just want to be working. The world of 'handmade' and crafting has

come a long way with pricing and marketing since, and now I know I can make a great living from doing what I love. In 2015, I started teaching home educated children to knit and crochet, and in 2018 I taught my first adults to crochet. 2019 will see the launch of my online teaching."

"Aside from all that I had another baby somewhere along the way, and together with my husband, who's now a qualified horticultural specialist, we home educate all 3 girls. 2019 will also see me qualify in aromatherapy and crystal healing, and a whole new chapter of life will begin."

NANCYE FROM NANCYEARTIST

"I always loved art as a child and whilst all hell was breaking loose all around me, I found solace in art. My art teacher was an inspiration as she was the only adult that really listened to me. I always wanted to study art but was told by my adult people that it would never earn me a living. So, I went into design and moved over to The Netherlands to study a BA in Design. After graduating, I went into health care for people with mental illnesses and aimed to combine my art to become an art therapist."

"Roll on 2009 and after a traumatic day at work I became suddenly very ill. I started having terrible nightmares every night and found it hard to concentrate and felt exhausted and anxious. When things became too much for me to bear and I didn't want to go through it anymore I was admitted into hospital on a ward for people with mental illnesses. I stayed there a month whilst they tried to sort out some kind of medication for me. Unable to work, I tried to find some sort of hobby to keep me busy whilst I was staying there. I finally found a place where they made art. So, I went, feeling anxious but quite quickly picked up my pencils and ended up designing my own pattern. Pretty much where I had left off at college. I was told to do what I wanted, what did I want to make? And so, began my journey into all that glitters."

"Three years later I was diagnosed with Complex Post Traumatic Stress Disorder as a result of my childhood and the family life I experienced. It turned out I had been suppressing all my memories and feelings until it literally exploded out of me. I entered into a long battle of therapy and learning again how to live, to love, to survive in a positive way. Meanwhile I continued on my journey of making new art and it started to develop into what it is now.

My art style is now bursting full of colour, is terribly glittery and is made by that little girl within who was denied her childhood and who is now learning every day, to play, have fun, live life and love with her happy little heart."

VICKI FROM CREATIONS – WHERE IDEAS COME ALIVE

"Growing up I was never really that interested in crafting despite my one nan and my mum both knitting, crocheting and sewing. I was diagnosed with epilepsy from the age of 8 and I was more interested in books than dolls and so became a bookworm reading about Stig of the Dump or the Adventures of Narnia (I still have my original books) or taping the Top 40 on a Sunday!"

"However, when I started working with two ladies at the age of 16, I discovered the world of cross stitch embroidery and they taught me how to get started. Well that is when I became hooked and my crafting journey began with various kits being brought to life, most of which still hang in my parents' house!"

"As time went by, I started making cards and years later when I became a mum, I used to entertain myself by crafting of an evening when my kids were snuggly tucked up in bed."

"In 2010, I took a huge decision to end my 17-year relationship with my partner as he had put me through three years of mental abuse and one day, I just could not take it anymore! Shaking as I heard the key turn in the lock, knowing he would have been drinking, I knew this was the day I had to make changes for my own sake and that of my kids!"

"Adjusting to be a single mum of two young children was the toughest thing I've had to go through. I lost my mojo for crafting as being both mum and dad, doing school runs, shopping, housework, etc I was too tired to craft, I would just curl up on the sofa, staring blankly at the same four walls surrounding me night after night. It was then I decided I needed to get back into creating and make better use of those evenings."

"I still went into networking groups around social media and saw lots of gorgeous jewellery makes and decided I wanted to try to make my own jewellery. I started by going to the library and getting out books on creating jewellery, I bought a few tools and some beads and find-ings etc and watched numerous YouTube video tutorials. Soon I was creating gorgeous bracelets. I then started to wear some of the jewellery I had made, and I started to feel confident again and realised it was exactly what I had needed. I had found a purpose again. So, on 28th December 2013, I launched my business."

"As well as beads I also love to work with epoxy resin creating colourful pendants in all sorts of shapes and sizes. I also make gifts such as keyring, bookmarks, bag charms, cufflinks and I'm sure it won't stop there."

"My aim today is to create stunning jewellery to help women feel confident to go out there and be themselves and know that YOU are enough, and YOU are strong, and no-one can keep YOU down!"

Vicki is one of the incredible Madmin team and she helps with our shopping live streams and is preparing to launch a podcast too!

Vicki also writes some incredible blogs and she has kindly allowed me to use one off of her website which really fits into sharing the love.

International Women's Day – 8th March 2019

What better way to celebrate 3 amazing women in my life than on International Women's Day.

Firstly my mum: At the age of 55 my mum was deeply into her crafts, having enrolled on floristry and cake decorating courses, learning about sugar craft and she was really excited. Then she was diagnosed with what we hoped was Carpel Tunnel but was in fact Parkinson's Disease. It was a complete shock for us all, but my mum has from then until now, some 10 years later, never let it stop her from doing what she enjoys. She turns her hand to all kinds of crafts, baking, cake decorating, card making, knitting, crochet, random projects she has seen on Facebook, you name it she will try it, sometimes to our amusement. I still laugh at the rather large snowman she made out of plastic cups! It was like an episode of Blue Peter! She is strong and will do anything for us girls. My mum is my Inspiration!

Secondly my youngest sister. As a family, we were all very excited about the new identical twin boys who were about to come into the world. My own daughter, my first child had been born 5 months before. I still remember the call I got off my mum whilst I was on my way to work that April. She told me my sister had gone into labour. She was early, not due for another month. I assured my mum it would be okay, to be told but it's not okay, she lost one of the babies. I lost a nephew that day, but my sister lost her son. We were all devastated, shocked, but we got through it and my sister was so brave. I can't begin to imagine how she felt that day losing a child. Adam is never forgotten and is spoken about often. His Twin turns 16 this April and he also has a 13 year old younger brother. They are wonderful lads, hard working and kind. My sister is my Inspiration!

Finally, my middle sister. She was the first to have a baby – he is now 17 and is taller than me by far. He has faced struggles, found it hard to make friends and has dyslexia. Despite his struggles he passed his exams, enough to get him onto his Art course at College. He is the most wonderful young man and dotes on his younger siblings. Then there is my niece who was diagnosed with Aspergers and again struggles with day to day emotions and feelings. She has good days, bad days and very bad days. Then there is my youngest nephew who has

Autism, attends a special needs school and is classed as non verbal. I say classed as non verbal, but every day he finds new ways to communicate, whether that is using Makaton signing or chattering away and communicating with us in his own ways. He loves to sing and knows all the words to all the songs in The Greatest Showman. This is Me reduces us to tears! These kids are achieving so much because of one person, their mum, my sister. She is also my Inspiration.

So, it is no wonder that with these 3 inspirational women by my side, that when I had cause to be strong and leave a 17 year relationship when it turned mentally and emotionally abusive, I knew I could do it! I am now a single mum, with 2 gorgeous kids, working full time and running a business.

This International Women's Day, I salute all women out there. I am now my kids inspiration!

Sharing the love is my favourite chapter and will help inspire or motivate anyone who is having a tough day.

THE RISE OF THE PHOENIX

One of my favourite stories is that of the phoenix. Even though this is not business related, I truly believe that everything happens for a reason and that one day we will all have the chance to rise from the ashes! The rise of the phoenix symbolises transformation, death, and rebirth in its fire. As a powerful spiritual totem, the phoenix is the ultimate symbol of strength and renewal. As a child, I loved to read stories that related to the phoenix but over the years I had forgotten about how inspiring they were and how it made me want to live each day to the fullest, especially after my Dad died.

The next time I heard a mention of the phoenix was by Stacey Sargison, who talked about the phoenix in relation to herself, women in general and how far she had come. Those feelings of holding my head up high when I was judged and talked about (I had been told that I had wasted my life, when I became such a young mother and that I could have gone to university and made something of myself) soon came flooding back. I have followed Stacey for a few years now and I have learned a lot from her. I also belong to her Facebook group, The Human Connections, which is full of phoenixes and inspirational women.

HEARTIZAN - HOW TO UPSCALE YOUR BUSINESS

- Never give up – it can be so easy to throw in the proverbial towel, but nothing happens overnight and we have to put in the hard work.
- Reach out to your tribe or supporters and ask for help.
- Look into passive income like a course or an affiliate programme.
- Collaborate with other creative businesses.
- Launch a new product and generate excitement.
- Send out emails with a special offer or a sale.
- Create a lead magnet.
- Sell off your old stock and launch your new products.
- Build relationships with not only creatives but other businesses too.
- Let go of the past as it will only hold you back.
- Remember everything happens for a reason and the best is yet to come.
- Stay on track and don't deviate from your plans, goals or dreams.
- Stop people pleasing.
- Develop a thick skin.

- If you don't want to do something say NO.
- Show up consistently.
- Become an expert in your field.
- Your cheerleaders will follow you; make sure you show your gratitude often.
- Write blogs about each other or even post them on your own websites.
- Share the love (pages, social media posts, YouTube, offers and competitions.
- Your will find your own tribe and the right people will rise up with you.
- Consider wholesale and outsourcing.
- Go offline and network with other businesses, it is so easy to stay online but when entrepreneurs and business owners get together, amazing things happen!

HEARTIZAN FAMILY

This chapter is all about the team behind the marketplace, how I met them, either online or in person, and how we all have the same hopes, dreams, challenges and how we have come together to help others. Everyone has a story which needs to be heard and we need to start sharing them; people buy from people and the more we are visible, the more people will remember us and our stories and what we sell. Most sales of handcrafted items are based on emotion; the buyer has connected with the seller or the products. Tapping into people's emotions as well as solving a problem for them will help you make sales.

You need to get out of your own way too, which sounds a little rough but dump those negative thoughts in the bin and move forward with gusto. We have discussed the damage a negative mind set can cause and how to become a lot more positive and for me this (as I have previously mentioned) started with Facebook live-streaming. These began with my story, a demonstration showing off my products and a competition. My children also went live; they don't have hang ups like we do and all of my children (the younger ones) wanted some of that airtime!

I am dedicating this entire chapter to the wonderful creatives from

Heartizan who have given up their time and faced their fears to put their stories into words, to be included in our book.

VICKI SMITH – CREATIONS – WHERE IDEAS COME ALIVE

Vicki is such a warm and lovely member of the team and has a very wicked sense of humour. She joined Heartizan way before our marketplace was born and our admin duties were to help another Facebook page to get seen. We did this by commenting on their pages every day. Vicki has helped to organise these groups of businesses, post reminders and then in time, when we launched our own Heartizan page, she also helped with that.

We used to run a competition for businesses called The Heartizan Eye and our lovely Vicki would go live and announce the winner every Sunday.

Now Vicki is part of the Marketplace team where she helps creatives list their beautiful handmade products and she also allocates them to each Madmin. She also helps to run The Artisan Toolbox group along with her own business, a full-time job and a single parent to two gorgeous children. Vicki is one busy lady!

I met Vicki at the NEC in Birmingham; I had been chosen by Theo Paphitis to exhibit at the Autumn Fair, so she visited me there. Meeting someone in real time, when you have known them for a long time online, is a feeling that is hard to explain. You know them well; you live stream with them and chat a lot too! It is like meeting up with a family member that you haven't seen in a long time; you hug and feel part of that person's life and then talk like you haven't been apart!

Here is Vicki's story:

"I set up my business in 2013 after a very stressful time and after leaving a mentally and emotionally abusive relationship. I needed something to fill the evenings and my crafting was taking over my home, so I decided to try to sell some of it. At the time I made cards

because I got bored of the cards, I found in shops that were all the same and so started up a Facebook business page. I joined lots of networking groups and started to see my page grow. I then started moving into jewellery making as well as wearing my own jewellery after my experience improved my confidence. Now, I want other women to look and feel great and confident going about their day-to-day life. I absolutely love it. I've learnt a lot along the way about business and continue to see my business grow."

ANGELA PICKHAVER – ALL STITCHED UP AND GAWJUS GIFTS

Angela joined us last year as part of the Madmin Team. She is incredibly talented and a big team player. She quickly became a team leader and does a fabulous job of organising the page and the Madmin roles. She works tirelessly and is a huge asset to Heartizan.

"A little background history – I didn't have a good start to life, suffering years of emotional, physical & sexual abuse. My road into business started after a very rocky road had been travelled. Once I had taken early retirement from nearly two decades of being a chef, I was suddenly in a position of no job & raising 2 children (I had been divorced for years). Well, depression, anxiety & addiction took their toll. Eventually, I went into a spiritual retreat for over 9 months for lots of intensive therapy. After leaving, I took courses in NLP & counselling, I did volunteer work for the local Woman's Aide Refuge and many other things to improve our lives. However, whilst waiting to hear about a job I'd applied for I had a moment of clarity & decided that I needed to have a life & job that really meant something to me. So, I did a bit of market research & made my own flyers for the sewing alterations business. A lot of literal 'footwork' happened putting these everywhere I could, including neighbours' doors, the local shops, etc. Once I started getting interest & jobs, I decided to make a website, advertise online anywhere that was free & this included Facebook. I was delighted & the business went from strength to strength. Jump forward to 2016 when my partner & I became full- time carers for his

mother, Joyce, who had dementia. We had to move too, enabling us to have the extra space for her needs. However, this also meant that I had to reduce the amount of sewing work I could do. Once Joyce passed away, I was suddenly left with more time but less clients & to get through the grieving I began to decoupage & make jewellery as a hobby. This sparked my creative juices & my ambition to become a successful businesswoman. Hence 'Gawjus Gifts' was founded & my products were being sold both online & at a local Hand- made Craft Shop. Now I have both of my businesses under one umbrella & a bright future ahead of me."

LAURA JAYNE - SQUDGE CRAFTS

LJ joined us way before the marketplace was launched and even though she is very unwell she keeps her chin up and is so supportive to others. LJ helps out in the comment groups and does a fabulous job!

"For years I have struggled with chronic pain and I searched for ways to help with the pain. One day, a lady at a festival gave me a braid to do. I tried it and then forgot about it for a month or two. When I found it again, I discovered that it distracted my brain for a bit. I spent ages braiding and ended up with meters of braids. One friend suggested I turn them into bracelets. That's when the jewellery started. I discovered beads and other exciting additions. I spent a few years creating exciting and beautiful jewellery purely for a family festival I go to each year. I started going to craft shows and saw a lady creating cards. I got a flashback to making cards with my nan as a child and then my addiction with papercraft was reignited. I adore making cards and jewellery because I love being able to help people send little bits of love to their friends and family. I was looking to grow my page and wanted to join a craft group, a friend introduced me to Heartizan, and it was fantastic. So many creative people with so much knowledge. Before long I joined the madmin team because I wanted to give back and support other crafters. I love this community, and I love how I can now buy hand-made gifts for all my friends and family. Crafting helps me in so many

ways, pain relief, positivity, a creative outlet and a connection to a wonderful community of crafty geniuses. I am looking forward to growing even more and developing new skills."

JESS LANCASTER – JILL AND JESS JEWELLERY

Jess joined us not long after she won one of our challenges; she was so excited to have won and I loved her enthusiasm. We met on one of Jules' Live it, love it, sell it workshops and she is just as fabulous in person. Jess helps with many functions within the team and is now working on our Facebook page.

"How Jill & Jess Jewellery was born... Hi there, I'm Jess, one half of the duo that is Jill & Jess Jewellery. Back in 2010, I started going out with Jill's eldest son (eldest of three); with that came spending more time with his parents to "get to know them". Jill was always busy making bracelets and earrings with beads on the sofa for friends. With wanting to get to know her a bit more, I started to help which soon grew to be Jill teaching me the basics of jewellery making. I learnt about the different types of braids, knotting techniques and the differ-ence between glass and semi-precious gemstones. As I became more involved and started to figure out that I loved to use wire and semi-precious gemstones, my collection of materials started to grow and grow. It is now about 1/2 the size of Jill's (two sheds, a conservatory and the lounge/dining room) although she does have a few years on me. My favourite items to make are wire rings and wire flowers, both with semi-precious gemstones. I have not seen these around very much especially due to me needing them a little bigger than the average size. This is not a full-time job for either of us as I work full-time as a resource assistant and Jill hasn't worked since her eldest (nearly 29) was born. Making jewellery is something that keeps us both busy; it also helps me to relax and de-stress from work. There is nothing better than manipulating wire to take the stress out of my day. We sell on Facebook and at a couple of smallish fairs a year as well as having an Instagram account and selling with Heartizan, of course. I would say

that to start with it was for friends and family until we went on a couple of courses to refine our skills. Heartizan is the reason that our business is ever growing! I took a risk by asking to be added to the comment groups (to grow the business) and I am so glad that I did; it has been truly fabulous for us. Well, eight years later we have created a small but growing business that is still a hobby for both of us and without complicating anything we kept the name simple: Jill & Jess Jewellery."

DALE PATRICK EVANS – PICK 'N' MIX GIFTS

Dale won an upgrade during our launch party and I asked him to join our team not long after. He is our only male Madmin and is our fabulous King of Chocolate! He has an incredible business and makes chocolate to die for! Dale helps us with the marketplace amongst lots of other tasks!

"I started my business when I was only 17 years old and since then have kept growing. I started out making sweet cones and sweet trees for parties but since then have expanded to have my own sweet cart and Krispy Kreme cart and I also design and decorate cakes for all celebrations. In October 2017, I started making handmade chocolates. I started with just a single flavour of truffle and have since grown my range of chocolates to include 15 different flavour truffles and a range of other chocolate gifts and treats, even starting my own subscription box in January 2019. I started my business because I have always had a flair for working for myself and I am very motivated to do well. I was also a DJ from the age of 13, which I gave up a few years ago when Pick 'n' Mix got busier. I started my business to try to prove other people wrong as I was bullied most of my school life and left school and sixth form with very little confidence and low self-esteem. But by running my own business, I have become more confident and since finding Heartizan my confidence has grown even more. I am very determined to do well and if someone tells me that I can't do it, it makes me want it even more and work even harder to achieve it. I have

big goals for the future which I thought were far away but since looking into them more, they are a lot closer than I expected and I'm hoping that I will be running my dream business and working for myself within the next year. Eekk.

I have had a few knock backs in my business from failed products, lack of motivation and even times of giving it all up. However, there are plenty of high moments which make it all worthwhile and you have to take the lows with the highs and keep going. Never give up on your dream. I am now very close to achieving my dream and that's because I have never given up and have always worked though the low moments and come out the other side."

AMY SEARLE – RAINBOW POOCHY

Amy joined us this year after smashing one of our live challenges. She is an amazing lady who has survived so many struggles and still has a huge big smile on her face! Amy helps in quite a few teams and is now a lead too, she is incredible and continues to amaze me!

"I was born with a spinal curvature and defect in my hip called sacroiliac joint displacement which means my tendons never bonded on the side of hip. which causes me difficulty walking. Between the ages of 7 and 12 I had several operations on my knees due to the fact that when I was born my knee cap wasn't set in the proper place. The operation on my knees had caused me to get juvenile arthritis when I was 12. This caused me to be in a wheelchair for a year due to walking being too painful, but I never gave up, I wanted to walk. So, every day I stood up and tried to take a step and most days I fell down but I again I never gave up and eventually I taught myself to walk again. I finished schooling, went to college and started working in care. At the age 23/4ish I had spent 5 months of work due to poor health and the doctor told me enough is enough and medically retired me. I went from working a lot of hours to nothing. I picked up my card making again as I used to craft with my mum and auntie when I was young to stop the depression setting in and the boredom. I set up a little business selling

handy crafts; this business ran for around 6 years. As my health got worse, I struggled to complete orders and some crafts were causing me too much pain. I kept trying until October 2017, when I was involved in a motorcycle accident and broke my pelvis in six places. My dream was to ride a motorbike before my legs got worse, which I achieved. I was in hospital for 6 weeks and bed bound for 6 months.

I decided to carry on making dream catchers as these didn't cause me any pain and I enjoyed making them. My friend offered to sell them for me on her trade stand and they then became her best seller. I felt like I had purpose again even from my bed. I had a really bad day one day; my medication wasn't touching the pain and I was crying for my mum like any grown woman of 32 would do. My daughter was six at the time and she came home from school, gave me a cuddle looked at me and said something that will stay with me and inspire me for the rest of my life, she said "tonight mum I'm going to grow". I replied with a brave face as I didn't want her to see how much I was in pain, telling her that every night she grows, it's what you do when you're young. She said, "No mummy I'm going to grow my legs so you can have them so you can be free of pain". This was the wake-up call I needed, the push to say you can do this. I sat and spoke to hubby and we looked at crafts I could do that wouldn't hurt me. I came across decoden and fell in love with how quirky it was; it suited my love for kitsch and unusual items. The same with the duct tape crafts; I thought they were so different. So, I did my research over the next few months while laid up. Hubby helped me come up with the name and we decided that it had to include the word rainbow as I have had rainbow hair for many years and the poochy came about as I want to launch a pet range as have made toys for friends and they were well received. I officially launched Rainbow Poochy in November 2018 and I haven't looked back. I have learnt from my failures and have a good support around me. I found Heartizan in February and like most was nervous of internet platforms due to being burnt before. I did my research, followed them on Facebook and YouTube and asked lots of questions which they were happy to answer, and I then joined. I haven't looked back; the team are amazing and so supportive and helpful. My attitude to life is to never give up. My health does not define me it is just something I was dealt with; it can't be changed but with a good mental attitude I can control it rather than it controlling me. I will carry on inspiring my daughter and show her never to give up on your dreams and that no matter what life throws at you there is always a way through things."

CLAIRE AUSTIN – BIRDCAGE CREATIONS

Claire is new to business and joined Heartizan through a friend and not long after she joined the team too! She juggles a business and children and is totally amazing!

"I launched my business in February 2019. I started my crafting journey after my son was born. I thought I would like to start making candles for my own use for a hobby and a bit of me time. I did enjoy it, however at the time, they were a bit hit and miss and didn't also turn out the way I wanted. I didn't realise there was such a science behind making candles and it was hard to master. I met an old work colleague at a local craft fair, told her I was making candles and she had loads of candles supplies she no longer wanted, so she offered to sell them to me. I brought them off her and discovered she had two businesses and we had loads in common. I mention her because I would not have ever started my business without her. She has given me so much, she's my best friend, mentor and has always supported me. I never realised I wanted to start my own business until our friendship started and she has been my rock throughout all the hard things life throws at you. She is always there for me and has given me so much advice on starting my business and has given me the confidence to go live. I cannot thank you enough Karly (Bow Cottage and Piccalilli Lane, a little plug!) and also my family for believing in me and supporting me on my journey, which is just beginning. I feel like I have never been this happy before. I don't mind the long hours, hard work and getting the family balance right. I'm my own boss, I can look after my children and hopefully be a good wife to my wonderful husband. So, I made candles for a while. Not

long after this, my husband and I decided to get married. We didn't have a lot of money and were working on a tight budget.

So, I made all my invitations, table plan, décor for venue etc. I decided I would make my own wedding favours to save money and I had all this wax, fragrance etc. I thought I wouldn't make candles as problems could occur and I didn't want to burn anyone's house down. So, I decided to make wax melts. I made about 40 tins, full of mini wax melts and I got loads of amazing feedback. So, I started to practise and research. I asked friends and family to test them until the formula was right. I found out I was pregnant with my second child and my son was diagnosed with autism; I am also his carer. I set up in business when I was on maternity leave. This was not a hard decision to make as I worked full time and in a different town, which was a 30 minute drive away. I wanted to be close to my children, look after my own children and also couldn't afford the big childcare costs. I love my new job; it makes me so happy and I'm doing what I love each day and bringing my children up the way I want to, and they are so happy and that makes me happy. My husband didn't want me to go back to my full-time job as I regretted it so much when my son was younger, and it did feel that my job came before my child and husband to be. I just couldn't do it again; the thought of it made me sick! So, this is why I set up my business.

Making wax melts is my true calling in life, I love making my customers happy and customer service is my number one priority (for my old job, I worked in customer service for years). I have a massive passion and so many ideas to develop my brand and I want to make my company as big as possible and offer services you cannot receive with a normal wax vendor. I decided to call my Business 'Birdcage Creations' as my centrepieces for my wedding were birdcages. I was going for a vintage theme. Originally it was going to be called 'Birdcage Crafts.

However, my friend said it would sound better being 'Birdcage Creations' as it sounds more professional. Also, I didn't want to pigeonhole myself into just one area, as I want to expand my business into other areas later down the line. I launched my business about a month ago and I have had a few sales, and I have gone live on the Heartizan page, which I never thought I would ever do. I have lots of new products I want to list and so many ideas on what I would like to create next. Once my Heartizan shop is fully set up and up to date, I will be looking into another platform to sell on. Also, I want to learn more about Twitter and Instagram as I'm pretty new at this and want to improve number of followers. I also want to set up a Pinterest account.

A friend introduced me to Heartizan, a new selling platform/marketplace with loads of support and advice. I love it! For a total newbie like me, this has given me the confidence to go out of my comfort zone and push myself and my business. I have even gone live; I never thought I would have the confidence to do this without Heartizan's/the Madmin's encouragement and support. I cannot wait for the future and I am so happy, I'm going on this journey with so many amazing people and Heartizan.

The most important thing for me when starting my business was a good product; branding is key, as is marketing and networking. A good product is so important. You have to offer something no one else is offering or have something special about your product. I have gone for luxury. I use the finest fragrances and wax. I also have large diamond

heart wax melts and I will soon be launching birdcage wax melts as part of the range. I believe branding, logo and product photos are key to a successful business. It's worth paying for a good logo (I paid £35, so not that expensive). I wanted a birdcage, two birds and a vintage theme. Photos of your products tell a lot about your business and product; use clear photos with a lovely background. Set your company from the rest out there. You can also use props, however, make sure this doesn't take your eye away from your product.

ANGELA RAMSDEN – DOLLY ROCKER

Dolly joined us this year and she is also a Madmin lead in the market-place team. She is happy, enthusiastic and a fabulous businesswoman. She was my accountability buddy for this book and without her I wouldn't have finished it within our timescale. She made me a vision board, collated everyone's stories and has kept me on track. We will be meeting up in the very near future!

"We are a partnership of myself Angela and my older sister Gillian. We are based in Manchester and are mums to five healthy, if somewhat crazy, children. We have always been creative and love making gifts for people, clothes and furnishings. We mainly sold our products at fayres and through word of mouth and did really well but with five children and life in general, finding the time was difficult. In 2016, we lost our dad suddenly and our world totally fell apart. For some time, mum, Gill and myself were lost, just surviving day by day, then one day I decided to get my sewing machine out again. It was a present from my dad and I just felt the need to use it again. I sewed and sewed into the early hours and totally escaped the sadness that had engulfed me since dad died. The next day I told mum and Gill about it and that's where it all began Crafting is our form of therapy and we love to spend the

day working together with mum helping too. We initially just sold on Facebook and Instagram and as our following grew so did our orders. It was chaos so we needed a way to streamline the order process. We found other handmade sites very expensive and impersonal and after taking a look at Heartizan we took the plunge and it's the best thing we have ever done! Within 24 hours of joining we were contacted by a REAL person who helped us get set up. She answered all our questions, gave us tips and was dedicated to us. We had our first sale within 48 hours of opening our shop! With the support from Heartizan, tips and challenges given to us, we have gone from strength to strength. Our hope for the future is to increase our online sales and be stocked in three shops within 12 months and spend as much time with mum as possible. The long-term goals are for my sister to finish work and join me on a full-time basis and make our dad proud."

LISA LUCAS – BY HOOK, BY YARN, BY LISA

I have met Lisa a few times, way before Heartizan was launched through my Cuddle Bed business. We connected through a group on Facebook and met at an event at the Ritz which was just fabulous! Lisa is a photographer as well as an amazing creative and has also taken my professional photographs.

"I've always been a knitter. My mum taught me how to knit and crochet when I was a youngster. I have vivid memories of her boxes of the most colourful yarns as she created gorgeous blankets made up of small granny squares. But knitting took over and that's what I loved. Recently I joined a friend at a knitting and crocheting group and watched with interest as other members were crocheting things other than granny squares. I decided to give it another go. Slowly but surely, I got back into the swing of crocheting and became completely addicted to it.

At around the same time as rediscovering a love of crochet, my brother's health started to take a turn for the worse. He already lived with kidney failure and dialysis but was then diagnosed with cancer in August 2017. Looking back now, I think my crochet helped me beyond words to deal with this major trauma in my personal life. I was working on a blanket at his bedside on the evening that he passed away. By Hook, By Yarn, By Lisa came into being towards the end of 2018. I was filling the house with blankets of all sizes, and it seemed like it might be a good idea to try selling my creations. There really are only so many blankets the cats need.

The opportunity came along to join Heartizan with my own little page, and I decided I had nothing to lose. I'm still refining my niche, but I think it'll be mostly blankets. I look forward to growing my little business and providing customers with amazing creations, most of which will be unique to them. I prefer to make items bespoke rather than having piles of stock, and I think that makes the items even more wonderful to have. I'd very much like to work with them to create blankets for dialysis patients. From my brother's experience, I know that patients can get rather chilly whilst dialysing and a simple blanket can help."

NANA SUE – BUTTON BUDDIES/NANA SUES EMPORIUM

Sue is an amazing business lady and is part of our top package. She has made such an incredible product for her granddaughter Matilda and is helping so many other children too. We all love our Nana Sue!

"When did Button Buddies start? Unknown to us all at the time – January 2008 – the twenty-week scan included those dreaded words "Spina Bifida". We had no idea what an enormous rollercoaster ride the family was heading for. Matilda Sue was born on the 24th May 2008 weighing 5lbs 2oz, Matilda's biggest hurdle. Her first major surgery, back closure, was at three days old, and she then went on to spend the next eighteen months in and out of hospital spending several months at a time due to her very complex related health issues, one of these being epilepsy.

Matilda was, and is, a very strong-willed little girl and from a very young age just would not take any medication without a major fight on our hands. Many nurses thought Mummy and Nana were too soft, so we said here's the syringe "off you pop you try". After not very long, Matilda wore medical staff down and the decision was made to have a feeding tube fitted so we could medicate effectively. Many people develop a sensitivity to medical gauze, as did Matilda quite quickly, and sticking plaster was needed around the "peg site" area to absorb natural leakage. So I researched an alternative and after many trials came up with my unique multi-layered recipe for a solution: bamboo terry (for the base next to the skin) made from natural bamboo fibres and rich in natural anti-bacterial and anti-fungal properties and super absorbent – an ideal medium for my specific requisites with added benefits too. An inner core of 100% cotton wadding, again for absorbency.

All that was needed now was a fun aspect to bring a "smile" to the wearer and pride to show off their very own button accessory and this is where the Button Buddie Critters came into their own – critters such as "Freddie the Frog", "Hettie the Hedgehog", "Walter the Whale", Duckie, Teddies, Cats, Butterflies and the critter family continues to grow. The Button Buddie seed began to germinate. Matilda's teddy pad was seen for the first time by a Specialist Nurse in Manchester Children's Hospital on her rounds one day – this lady loved them and began showing them around the wards. Word quickly spread of Matilda's peg companion and that little seed from that very day began to grow.

Now we had a Button and a Buddie, my very own business naturally sprang out: "Button Buddies". It was a truly amazing start of a journey which has quickly grown month on month. It is my intention to continue to bring a little joy, a little comfort to those people who find themselves needing a feeding tube for whatever reason. Each Button Buddie is sewn with much love and care. Who knows what the future holds for Button Buddies? But as sure as day follows the night, I won't stop making them for these very special people in our lives."

DEBBIE EDWARDS – PAPERCUTS AND PAWS

Debbie is another new Madmin and helps us on the page and in the comment groups. She is a fabulous lady who works incredibly hard and juggles lots of hats!

"I relocated to Cambridgeshire in 2016 and was fortunate to only need to work part time. I had lots of time to spare so my business started as a hobby first. Then as I became more confident, I started selling via FB and craft fairs in April 2017. My name was chosen because I started out with paper cutting and my love of dogs. I have two spaniels. I now make hand painted MDF gifts for all occasions, light-up bottles and

jars and deep box frames. I look for customers using various social media platforms, FB, Twitter, Instagram and local selling sites."

EMMA EVANS – EM'S PAPERLOVE

Emma joined us when we were building up the Heartizan page. Her duties were scheduling the page and to interact with businesses. She has also helped us with Instagram and she now runs The Artisan Toolbox with Vicki and answers all the page messages. Not only that, she looks after me and books in all of my mentoring sessions. I would be truly lost without Emma; she is so hardworking even though she has had some truly challenging times.

"Hi, I'm Emma, I started with pain about seven years ago. I had gall-stones which needed removing but the pain never went away. I was back and forth in hospital every few weeks. They said I had nerve damage from the surgery and the pain would never go away. I was in tears all the time. I also suffer from fibro, ME, sciatica, depression, anxiety and the nerve damage in my stomach and back. Five years ago, I saw a talented artist who did a starter kit for papercutting and I thought 'why not?'. I had never done any crafts before. I was bed ridden for a while as sometimes I can't walk at all. So, I got the kit out and the minute I started cutting, I loved it and couldn't wait to cut more.

I've been cutting for five years now; it's my escape from pain and panic attacks. I also have the joy of test cutting designs for people but if asked I can do my own designs too. I have the most amazing husband who doesn't complain if I can't do anything. I don't know what I would do without him and my daughter. I've also been an admin for Heartizan for over two years. They are family and I think the world of them all."

FAY NILSSON – WORLD DELIGHTS

Fay recently joined us to help lead the Pinterest team; she is the amazing daughter of our fabulous Angela so we know she will be a perfect fit for Heartizan.

"I am Fay, the creator of World Delights. I have two wonderful boys; a lovely husband and I work full time as a care support worker. I am the lead on Pinterest for Heartizan. I've always been a crafter; I make a range of things from crocheted goodies and macramé wall hangings to recycled woven paper. Life hasn't always been easy, but hey that's life, you can laugh or cry and I choose to laugh."

KATRINA BENTON – CREATIONS BY A BUTTERFLY

Katrina joined Heartizan a few months ago and quickly became a fabulous part of the team. She is an amazing woman who can run a business, home school, is a wife and still finds time to help others!

"Since my very first day at school, I have been known as a butterfly – this is where Creations by a Butterfly started. Aged just four and a half, I had the most wonderful teacher, Mrs Horner, who I still have contact with all these years on. At the end of the first day of 'rising five' she called me a butterfly, and it has stuck to this day. Here I am over 25 years on, with my own little business and a name just perfect to express me and my creations.

Going through my years at school, I had very little interest in the core subjects. However, in the arts department or in the drama studios I became a completely different person. When it came to Year 9 and having to choose my GCSE subjects, I had to choose between art or drama, as to take both was seen as an easy option."

"I chose drama as I had no confidence in my drawing abilities or that I could ever do more than block colouring. After leaving school, I worked through various temping agencies, I did a lot of admin and

reception work, but this never made my wings flutter. In 2005, I met the most amazing man, who I am now lucky enough to call my husband.

My life became a little rocky in 2006. I had some health issues that caused me to lose my full-time job. After six months of me being unwell and various testing, I was informed that my chances of having children were very slim. However, my health was finally at a point I was able to return to work, and I once again got myself back into an office. In October 2006, I passed my driving test and I purchased my first car. Then a few days later I didn't feel right. Something in my head told me something was different with my body. Knowing what the doctors had told me, I thought there was no chance I was pregnant, but to put my mind at rest I took a pregnancy test. It was positive!

In January 2007, I lost my job during the probation period, so I was back to being a housewife. Bored through the days, I decided that I would make the birth announcements for our bundle due in June. Every time we went to a supermarket, there were craft items, I purchased everything I could. My mum told me not to get in too deep as it would cost a fortune! I promised Mr B that I would have one small box of craft stuff this stuck for a little while. Miss A arrived at

the end of June 2007, and once her birth announcements had gone out, I wanted more creativity in my life, so I made her christening invitations, which led to me creating our wedding invites. In six months, I had gone from one small box with card blanks and peel-offs, to a five-draw unit with coloured paper, stamps, inks, colouring pens and more.

Not long after our wedding day, life became hectic with Miss A being up on her feet and into everything, so crafting became an evening-only hobby. In 2009, the need to craft was stronger than ever. I started to attend classes at a local craft shop, visiting craft shows and the 'office under the stairs' became 'the craft room' – the computer was full of photos of ideas and creations I had made. I loved crafting whenever I could and really grew as an artist and a person. I felt relaxed when free colouring in little hedgehogs and cutting up paper. I had learnt to colour using more than just one pen at a time; decoupage became a firm favourite.

In October 2009, while 20 weeks pregnant with our second bundle, I was admitted to hospital with pneumonia. As this was the peak of swine flu, as a precaution I was placed in a side room alone – this gave me far too much time on my own. I spent a week in hospital, unable to leave the room and so I started thinking about what I really wanted to do with my life and being creative was the top of the list. April 2010 saw the safe arrival of Miss N, so once again I was back to full-time motherhood with two little people now – I still had my dream of being a full-time creative at some point in the near future.

In early 2011, I had a message from a friend asking if I would make her wedding invites. This is when Creations by a Butterfly became more than a dream. I decided to get myself set up with business cards, a Face- book page and registered with HMRC. I signed up for various local events for the next six months and got my head down to creativity. Since then I have fluttered my wings day and night to grow my little business on and offline. You will always find me with five or more projects on the go at once; that's the butterfly in me. My creativity has allowed me to learn so many techniques that have helped me to be the butterfly I am. My first passion will always be handmade cards, but now my creativity allows me to make a huge range of items from personalised baubles, paper cuts, book sculptures, patterns and more. Heartizan became a part of my life in 2019. Seeing various advertise-ments around Facebook and other social media I took the plunge to become part of the team."

VICKY BANNISTER – EXPRESSIVE GIFTS

Vicky is a fabulous member of the Heartizan team. She works tire-lessly helping in our Crafters Display group and is our event organiser. She also admins on another group and is a huge asset to us. I have been lucky enough to meet Vicky and she is just as fabulous offline as she is online!

"I left a career in finance just prior to having my son in 2011. Going from working full time 50-60 hours a week to being at home with a baby at 41 was a big change!! It is of course very rewarding, but very different! Once he started school, I planned to go back to work part time, but I knew I couldn't go back to my old job, as it just wouldn't work with family commitments, and my husband's job means he is often away.

I decided that working in a school could be good – often in my former career people told me I would be good at training and teaching, so I embarked on a home study course. I started volunteering in a local school, completed the course and sought agency work on the days I was available. The course had covered special educational needs, and I spent some time working in both mainstream and special schools. I absolutely loved helping and working with the children, but work for support staff was limited due to the many government cuts, the hours didn't fit in with travelling to my son's school, and I figured this was not going to pay the amount I expected (or needed) to earn to make it viable.

Reinventing myself again, I thought long and hard what I could do from home instead. The answer was staring at me from the storage boxes we had upstairs full of my child's scribbles and drawings. Why not think of a way these can be used practically and seen every day? So, I did some online research, taught myself how to use some fancy graphic design software and set up a Facebook page telling everyone my intentions. The name came from the very nature of what I did – the business is called Expressive Gifts, and the word expressive by defini-tion means "To effectively convey thought or feeling".

I started selling online, transferring children's drawings and hand-writing to different products as keepsakes. Whilst it's not a totally orig-inal idea, I strive to make it different in some way, whether through my processes, the end products, added extras, as well as excellent customer care. Customers often request custom work, and I wanted to be able to accommodate these as much as possible, whilst still making a profit. I started creating my own designs through new found skills, and other graphics that could be added to the handwriting work such as elements to represent a person's interests or hobbies, just to make them extra special and unique.

In April 2019, I won a Twitter award for my handwriting work, and continue to work on offering new products, seeking out trends and any gaps in the market. I joined Heartizan at the end of January 2019, and as a Madmin very shortly afterwards to help others and offer any support that I can. Their support network is fantastic, and I've met some wonderful people, and I've had increased social media exposure and much more! Juggling running a business with a household and young family is never easy, but I absolutely love what I do and have great satisfaction making items that mean something."

FIONA FRASER – PRETTY WEE THING

Fiona is one of our amazing creatives and I am looking forward to getting to know Fi and her business better soon!

"I am Fiona (Fi as I'm mostly known), the owner of Pretty Wee Thing. My crafting is my "down time" (which I used to otherwise fill with 'faffing' – spending time doing nothing of interest) when I'm not running around the country as a Risk Consultant. I have a young son, whom I adore, and two mad dogs who keep me busy. As well as that, I am a cub leader and I also play in a steel band. My take on flowers is reasonably abstract. I love colour and I love to paint and draw with different colours to make my flowers 'pop' on different coloured back-grounds! I also like to use a sprinkle of glitter on dandelions and wild-flowers. My interest in crafts over the years was inherited from my brilliant mother, grandmother and grandfather who could paint, sew, knit and crochet."

DONYA STOKES – PRU'S SHOES

Donya is so amazing; she has an incredible business and she is a fabulous business woman! I love her creations and I am happy to say I have met her in person too!

"I am Donya the owner of Prus Shoes. I'm a resin artist specialising in Bespoke Keepsakes. Everything I make is made specifically for you using a variety of materials from horsehair, animal fur, human hair, photographs, ashes, wedding flowers and horseshoes. I have even set horse teeth, beetles, moths and butterflies (there's not much I won't cast; if it's dry it's going in).

You may notice a horsey theme here, I own two horses myself: Pru, my Arabian ex-racehorse, and Thunder, my little Welsh mountain pony. Horses are actually how I started my resin journey – it's a funny story. Basically, I cut my horse's tail too short and it looked like he was wearing a thong, so thought I'd better do something with it as I felt so bad. My business is named after Pru for this exact reason (I also work with horse shoes so it ties in nicely).

I've been working with resin in the heart of rural Derbyshire for a year now and have grown my business to over 5000 page likes in this time, something I'm immensely proud of. I've learnt so much over this last year. I started out making small Heart Keyrings containing my own horses' hair and have progressed to setting whole bouquets and people's own horseshoes. I love how versatile resin is; the possibilities really are endless.

I really enjoy making to order and getting to know the stories and reason behind people having their keepsakes made."

SUE TIMCKE AND ALLIE MCCLELLAND – EARTHGEMS

Sue and Alison opened their shop not long after we launched, and they are a fabulous mother and daughter team. They make the most gorgeous jewellery and I should know as I have some! Sue has recently joined the Heartizan Team too!

"Hi, I'm Alison McClelland (Allie) and I'm the owner of Earthgems Jewellery. I am dyslexic so apart from being my co-worker in the business, my mum, Sue, is also my scribe and social media guru! So, with corrected spelling and grammar mistakes, here is my story! I am 38 years old and I have three children aged 23, 19 and 15. If you're trying to work it out, yes, I was very young when I had them! Due to being only 15 when I had my son, I had to give up my planned career in engineering and with help from my family concentrate on being a good mum. I married at 19 and had my two daughters, but unfortunately nine years later that marriage was over, and I went back to being a single mum for many years. I now have a wonderful partner, two lovely step-children and am about to become a granny!

I've always been creative and even as a small child I loved making things. I think this is due to my dyslexia; I struggle to express myself in the written word, so I compensate by creating art and craft instead (and talking.... a lot!) this was always nurtured and encouraged as my mum has always had creative hobbies (she talks a lot too – it's hereditary!). Over the years we have tried lots of things from art to creating greetings cards and we both love baking, but the jewellery making was always my favourite. I started with seed beads when I was a teenager, then we worked with gemstone beads and wire.

As the children got older and I got divorced, the jewellery making turned from a small hobby to a way of helping support the family, alongside many part-time jobs. Eventually we just had too much jewellery to wear ourselves, so in 2008 I registered as self-employed, so we could sell what we had made, and we became Earthgems. A few years ago, dad bought mum a new hobby kit for Christmas and we discovered metal clays! Now our jewellery making is our passion and joy and therapy all rolled into one. Over the last 10 years, the business has grown; from doing just a few local fairs, we are now booked most weekends in the summer for fairs all over the Highlands and we now supply four local outlets, as well as selling online. We have also branched out to do workshops in metal clay showing people how they can make their own jewellery and sharing our passion. We have recently received an award on Twitter as Queen of Metal Clay thanks to the encouragement of this wonderful Heartizan community. We love the support we get and we're looking forward to growing with them and really making something of our small business."

GEMMA SULLIVAN – GEMS BOUTIQUE

Gemma is one of our amazing creatives and I am looking forward to finding out more about her fabulous business!

"Hi, my name is Gemma. I own Gem's Boutique which I started in 2011 shortly after losing my nana, something to focus on while I was dealing with my loss. Actually, I wanted to make something from scratch, so she'd be proud of me as she was the lady who got me into sewing, recycling fabrics and having a 'waste nothing' attitude. I first started buying vintage clothing (before it got really fashionable), altering them to fit the modern lady. It was a dream, shopping every week looking for bargains.

With this, I got my first feature in Cambridge mag Style, and I was invited to take part in a fashion show at the Corn Exchange. My friend said how great this was. I remember making a joke "Next step Vogue, baby, Vogue!" The next month I was actually asked to feature in Vogue's vintage directory! I was over the moon!! Shortly after, I moved to London and attended fashions shows, and was in the BBC magazine! While all of this was happening, I was still working full time!!

I didn't have the confidence in myself to go ahead with Gem's Boutique fully! From 2013 to 2015, I wound down the vintage. As the high street jumped on the bandwagon, it was getting harder to compete, so I just dealt with 1920s and started taking on more seamstress work. Then in 2016, my body had given up; I woke one morning and couldn't move! I felt had been run over by a train! I was exhausted with daily chores and looking after myself. I couldn't do it any longer! I had ME/CFS – 2016 & 2017 were the hardest time of my life; everything had to stop! Including my little business, any work, social events! I had to take time out for myself.

Learning to manage my energy, everything had changed! But in 2018, I decided it was no longer going to beat me; I was going to learn to live and get the best out of my life! Funnily enough it gave me the confidence I had never had in my abilities to restart Gem's Boutique, to do it as a full-time job! Eight 8 months on, it's going better than I could have imagined, from strength to strength. Don't get me wrong, I still have daily battles with myself, but my Boutique gives me the flexibility I need. The support I get from Heartizan is amazing. They give me a little pick me up when it's needed; my madmin is second to none! My dreams for the future are to fully recover and take the world by storm."

SUE FRECKLINGTON – GRANNY MAUD AND THE OLD GRUMP

Sue joined as a creative selling her amazing items on our marketplace not long after we launched. She is an incredible lady who works tirelessly to help find a cure for AHC and she totally inspires me!

"Sewing is in my genes on both sides of my family! My mother was a dressmaker, my Paternal Great Aunt was a seamstress at Windsor Castle, and several generations have been workers of all sorts in the silk industry in and around Macclesfield. Some of my earliest memories are playing with the contents of my mother's button box, as she sewed on her treadle. Over the years, I had sewn clothes for family, but my first major quilt was a secret memory quilt for my daughter, made over 22 years from the clothes made for her by both mum and me.

Serious quilting was supposed to be a hobby for my retirement, but having supplied the family, I then had to look for another reason to sew. About the same time, we became aware of the rare illness of my penfriend's granddaughter, known as AHC (Alternating Hemiplegia of Childhood) for which there is as yet no cure. For two years, I helped to raise funds to find a cure by doing a yearly sponsored cycle ride. The final year was the distance between Lincoln and Reykjavik – over 1700m, but I did not like asking the same people every year to sponsor me, so I went back to the sewing, selling what I could at craft fairs, and teaching. This time with my husband's help, as he enjoys making things with wood.

Another of my handicrafts is crochet, and one month a magazine gave instructions for a Granny Maud square. As my middle name is Maud, it just had to be made (several of them, in fact, which became a warm jacket for cold venues), and this became my crafting name. When Tony needed a name to go with it, we toned down his original suggestion to the Old Grump.

My main challenges are not craft ones, but technical. Having been introduced to various sites by a crafting friend, eventually a connection was made with Heartizan. But networking and sales sites do not seem to work for me. I am very slow with the technology, and all the tasks leave me frustrated and bamboozled, as I do not know what I am doing wrong. It seems a waste of time that I could better use on making things, but what is the point of making things that I cannot sell?

My hopes and dreams are to be part of finding a cure for AHC! They are moving forward, but still there is much expensive work to be done. I would love to still be around when the cure is found.

Many years ago, in the Second World War, my Dad was stationed in Iceland. He was one of a group of soldiers lost in a snowstorm. He was rescued by an Icelandic family and they became firm friends. Sometime after he returned home, I was born and, in my teens, began a pen friendship with Gunny; it is her granddaughter, Sunna, who has AHC. In a way, I am paying back what they did for my family – after all without them I would not be here!"

BECKY CHANNING – MORE THAN A STITCH

Becky is a lovely lady who makes amazing crocheted and knitted items. My children have a fabulous hat and scarf set which is well loved.

"I started my business up about two and a half years ago. I was struggling to deal with day-to-day life due to suffering anxiety, depression and fear of going outside (open spaces). Knitting and crochet was my comfort to help keep me sane and my mind occupied. I decided to make it into a business.

I have osteoarthritis in both of my knees which I struggle with some days more than others. I can't always walk far, even though I do try; now I have managed to overcome the fear of going out. I have also suffered with my lower back for many years. I love what I do and the appreciation from my customers makes me smile and want to keep going and do more. I'm so glad I set my little business up, it's my baby and I'm loving watching it grow.

I love my Facebook page plus my Heartizan shop. Heartizan, with all the support help and advice I have been given from all the Madmins, has helped my business grow even more, I'd like to thank all at Heartizan for that as without them I'd not be where I am today. I do still have bad days with my depression and anxiety, but my work helps me through."

MICHELLE BEST – CHELLIE'S CREATIONS

Chellie is a fabulous creative and has just recently opened a shop with us.

"I am Chellie and I run a small business called Chellie's Creations. My business name is something I came up with because I am able to offer a wide range of services. I design, pattern draft, source fabric, manufacture and sell it all from my home in Lincolnshire. I have a degree in fashion and textile design and manufacture.

After completing school, I went to college and university and was the first woman in our family to get a degree. During the last months of my second year, I fell pregnant with my daughter and had her in the middle of my third year. I went back to university and finished my degree. I now also have a son. Since then, I have had some health problems which led to me leaving my last job and starting up my business. I have Bertolotti syndrome and a cyst in my spinal cord which is now seems to be affecting my bladder, bowels and kidneys and I am undergoing lots of tests.

In 2016, I lost my grandad, who was a role model and someone who I looked up to. I started my business in his memory as I know he would be so proud of me right now. I have been making clothes for my kiddies for years but in November I took the plunge and decided to start my own business. Since then I have had many exciting opportunities.

I make handmade clothing for children and adults. My best seller is the Bright Rainbow jumpers which I make for mummies, daddies and siblings. All my clothing can be adapted for children with sensory difficulties. I am able to make seams less bulky and I use soft fabrics.

I meet and work closely with families and children giving them a wide range of fabrics to choose from and this allows them to be made to measure. I also take time out of the children's wear side of my business to create costumes for photographers and models to wear to photo shoots; these are all designed and made by myself. I found Heartizan through Facebook. I signed up and I found the layout and the website was user-friendly. I absolutely love it and I'm so excited to be a part of a growing selling platform for handmade crafts."

NICOLA ARMSTRONG – LOVE ELLA JEWELLERY

Nicola is a wonderful new creative and has just recently opened her fabulous shop.

"Hi, I'm Nikki & I started Love Ella Jewellery towards the end of 2018 as I just love making jewellery. I've always dabbled in making bits &

pieces for myself over the years and I love creating new things. I suffer from anxiety and at times it can be really bad; I have found my jewellery making has been a great way to calm myself and just forget about everything. I started making more regularly, then some of my friends & family started asking me to make them bits. After getting some wonderful feedback I decided to go for it and try to sell some of my pieces.

I get lots of questions about the name I have chosen for my business. I named it after my daughter Ella, who unfortunately was born sleeping at 30 weeks. I never got to bring my beautiful daughter home with me, so I decided to name my little venture after her. I feel like it's my way of keeping her memory alive and keeping her close to me. Ella is in my mind every day, so it just felt right.

I came across Heartizan while I was researching different selling platforms and I am so pleased I signed up with them. Everyone is so positive and friendly. If you need any help with anything you only have to ask. It's so nice to feel supported."

JOYCE GUIBARRA – PINK SPOT CRAFTS

Joyce is a wonderful new creative and recently opened her fabulous shop.

"I'm Pink Spot Crafts. I am very new to crafting, but it has always been one of my loves. I love getting messy, making and doing. I've never been one to sit still, and now I have two kids, there's definitely no time for that! I was originally Pink Spot Photography, mainly shooting weddings. As amazing as this is, I have taken a big scary leap and decided to start my own craft business. There are two reasons for this – one, because it's a passion, and two, because I get to bring my children up and be at home for them. This is a big win for me as I feel so lucky to have that privilege! They love making too so it's great that they can get involved.

There's no great story as to why I'm called Pink Spot. I asked for a logo, and a pink spot is what I was shown. I loved the simplicity of it, and that's where my name was born. At the moment, I personalise glitter glasses. I love doing this. Glitter is a major favourite of mine. On the downside, it gets everywhere! On the plus side, my house is so beautiful and sparkly! I also transfer photos to wood. Having a love for photography, I didn't want to just forget all about it, so I still get to see everyone's beautiful photos and transfer them into wooden plaques, wood slices and wooden bunting. They make fantastic gifts and home decor.

My house is a shrine to my children. I have their photos hanging every-where! I can also engrave on wood. I make save the date wood slices, as well as keepsakes. This area of my craft will be constantly growing as my ideas progress and my product list expands. I can't wait for you all to see! So, what does the future hold for me? Well, I'm not asking to be rich, or make my millions selling my crafts. Although that would be lovely! All I want is to be happy and to be able to treat my kids when-ever I want to. This business is for them and their future. Any crafts I sell make my dreams come true but they also go towards making their dreams come true. If my crafts can make someone happy then that's my goal ticked right, there. I would of course like to be successful and like to be known for my crafts, and if that's only by a handful of people, well then that's an achievement, isn't it?

I found Heartizan by reading a Facebook post. I took a look, liked what I saw and signed up. I love the help and support I've had so far and have my fingers crossed that this will help make my future bright."

ELLEN HOGAN-FRANCE – GOODY TUTU SHOES

Ellen is another new creative but someone I knew previously from crafting groups. This lady is a true inspiration!

"My name is Ellen and I am a tutu addict! I have always been creative, even as a child I would customise my clothing to make it stand out. I always wanted to do something creative like be a fashion designer but

instead I had two kids, got married and went to university to train as a nurse. Sadly, my health took a turn for the worse and when my third child, my only daughter, was born, I started making her tutus, big bows and blinging up her tiny shoes. It was my favourite hobby when she was napping and as friends started commenting on them and showing interest in ordering for their own children, I thought why not give it a go and see if I can earn a few extra quid. Unable to work a normal full-time job because of multiple health conditions the idea of working for myself was very appealing, so when my daughter was 8 months old in September 2014, I launched my business Blinged by Ella-Bella and sold my very first tutu that same day.

I love everything sparkly so as well as tutus I customised shoes with sparkly crystals and made blingy Christmas decorations, glitter glasses and picture frames, among other items. After a couple of years and a few hundred tutus later I renamed my business Goody Tutu Shoes because I decided to focus on tutus and shoes. I concentrated on coming up with new dress designs and personalising tops to go with tutu sets. I bought myself a vinyl cutter and heat press and started selling personalised bags and clothing for babies to adult which has really widened my customer base as I can now offer something for everyone.

I needed an online store to get all my products organised and a few of my friends had joined Heartizan so I decided to give it a go.

It's only been a few months but it is going well and there is so much support and advice. I'm excited to get my shop filled up and continue adding new products. I love being my own boss and it doesn't seem like work because I love it so much, but this is my job and it fits in well with my life as a mother of three with chronic illnesses. If I need a few rest days I can take them. I've met lots of lovely people through my business; there is such a lovely community of crafters and handmade supporters. I hope I will be able to continue."

THE HEARTIZAN CREATIVE COMMUNITY AWARDS

Our creatives have learnt a lot implementing the Heartizan Way and here are some of their fabulous achievements:

HEARTIZAN

Small Business Sunday, WOW, Queen of Handmade Marketplaces Featured on Heart FM

CHRISSIE LOWERY – THE CUDDLE BED COMPANY

Winner of Small Business Sunday, Wow, Queen of Sensory Products, Smart Social, Winner of Dragonesses Den, Finalist of Best New Product – Networking Mummies, The StroudLife Business Awards Finalist and Highly Commended Business, Creative Biz Award, Winner of 6 Global Recognition Business Awards, Queen of 'Order of Fabulous', winner of a stand chosen by Theo Paphitis at The Spring and Autumn Fair. Winner of Women in Business.

Featured in Forbes, BBC, The Story Exchange, South West Business,

The National Autistic Society's magazine, The Lady Magazine, Sew and So, StroudLife.

The Echo (#21 new and up coming businesses to watch), The Spring and Autumn Fair magazine, SENS Resource Blog, Take A Break, That's Life, BBC Radio, TMDAC Biz Radio.

VICKI SMITH – CREATIONS WHERE IDEAS COME ALIVE

Queen of Resin Pendants, Smart Social, Creative Biz Award Featured on TMDAC Biz Radio

DALE PATRICK-EVANS – PICK N MIX PARTIES AND GIFTS

King of Handmade Chocolate, Smart Social, Small Business Sunday

AMY SEARLE – RAINBOW POOCHY

Queen of Dreamcatchers Featured in Club Hub

VICKY BANNISTER – EXPRESSIVE GIFTS

Queen of Handwriting Keepsakes, Wow and Small Business Sunday

ANGELA RAMSDEN – DOLLYROCKER

Queen of Fabulous and Functional

CARA VENN & LUCHEN VENN – PIROUETTE JEWELLERY DESIGNS

Queen of Gemstones Jewellery

SUE TIMCKE AND ALLIE MCLELLAND - EARTHGEMS

Queen of Metal Clay

SUE FRECKLINGTON - GRANNY MAUD AND THE OLD GRUMP

Featured in Quilting Magazine

DAWNLIZA - LAFRENIERE - THE SCENT OF A ROOM

Queen of Scented Relaxation, Twitter Sisters, Smart Social

DONYA - PRUS SHOES

Queen of Resin Keepsakes

DI WARD - BEE BELLES KEEPSAKES

Queen of Clothing Keepsakes, WOW, Woman in Business, Smart Social, H2H award for creative businesses

WORK IN PROGRESS

Heartizan was officially launched in September 2018 outside of our own Facebook groups. I have learnt a lot of lessons on how to run a business with a whole team of wonderful people but also a lot about myself too.

Heartizan was born out of helping others, which is very difficult to do when you need help yourself, something I find hard in all aspects of my life. During Heartizan's infancy, I was diagnosed with two more illnesses, all life-long and two degenerative. I know my health is deteriorating and I can do less and less; I am also becoming a much bigger person, literally! So, I have started to accept help from my team to allow growth of the company which I am now getting to grips with. Having two businesses is quite a challenge and I wrote a blog about that. I get a lot of inspiration and motivation from my children, my friends, my Madmins and my fabulous creatives, all of whom go through their own challenges, good times and bad times.

Blogs can help you get seen by google and are a good way to get your message out too, we all have stories that will resonate with others.

This is one of my blogs:

How hard can it be to write a book?

I sat at my desk to write this book and I thought exactly this; how hard can it be? Oh my word it is incredibly hard! I had to dig deep and try to process things that have happened to me and then write them down. I brainstormed to sort out the chapters with a very lovely close friend. I used my photos on my phone to remember the business journey that I have been on.

However, my why and the why of all the other stories that make up this book is much, much harder! I am a sensitive soul (not that I show that very often) and I have found that during the process I relived my demons and past difficulties along with sympathising with the other amazing people's stories too.

ACCOUNTABILITY

I do have an amazing team and one very lovely lady Dolly (Angela) helped me collate the stories and kept me accountable too, for which I am very grateful. I get easily distracted with Heartizan, being pulled here, there and everywhere and I also cannot sit for too long at my desk. I have degenerative spine problems, so I need to work on my mindset a lot!

We launched our crowdfunding campaign which was one big learning curve and a whole lot of work! My back became unbearable and I struggled to walk. I was trying to launch my new products for Cuddle Beds and also lead Heartizan. My mindset was not good, I was coming to terms with many issues. I have to admit, I felt like giving up, but I am not a quitter and I muddled through. I then received a call from London and Dragons' Den wanted me to attend an audition for Cuddle Beds in a short few days!

I was so excited, I had hope and a plan, I even worked on my exit plan so I could finally just manage one business and take that forward whilst my sensory items could be managed by my seamstress.

I was so excited, I had hope and a plan, I even worked on my exit plan so I could finally just manage one business and take that forward whilst my sensory items could be managed by my seamstress.

I had very little time to prepare, my website was not up today and my new products had not been launched, but I am a person who just does things, I feel the fear and I won't let it stop me. This mindset has taken me through my whole life and event thought the outcomes aren't always what I had hoped for, I still step into my power.

I truly believe my power is being visible, bringing like-minded people together and raising them up to feel powerful too so they can share their stories and become successful.

This was my second chance, I had first applied for Dragon's Den whist my business was in its infancy when I was not even trading, but I continued to apply. The next audition went so much better, I had a lot more confidence as doing live streams had helped me prepare a pitch.

I still didn't make it through, even after they phoned me several times and sent me numerous emails requesting more information. I did however have some wins that month too; I was featured in The Lady Magazine and I started wholesaling to Ireland, along with Robert Dyas and Wayfair.

Even though I didn't make it onto Dragons Den, I won another award and I had a radio interview as part of the prize. I then was nominated for a global award off the back of that interview and I ended up winning six Global Recognition Business Awards.

Information on the awards that myself and other creatives selling with Heartizan are in chapter six.

As all creative business owners know, the next launch, competition, award or collaboration is just around the corner

Heartizan is so much more than a marketplace; it is the heart and soul of an amazing community! The creatives of Heartizan are incredible people and they truly are like family. We help each other, we learn together, and we support each other. My team, who are now too numerous to name, work tirelessly and are worth their weight in gold. Heartizan will continue to grow, to help others and bring together more amazing creative businesses. Now we are getting the Heartizan name and our ethos out there to help other creatives really get seen and to bring online to offline. Our Heartizan plans are to hold workshops, events and to spread the word. I have days when I feel like I am going to give up, but I look at my children and I speak to my team and I know I can keep going.

All businesses are a work in progress, no matter how big or small they are and they will continue to evolve. Keeping on track even if the goals change is so important. Just like your products are a work in progress, so are your plans and if you continue to grow then that is a huge win.

My plans for writing this book changed when my health deteriorated but three months later the manuscript was written, edited and then published. I even have plans to write two more and those will be easier as I learned a lot with The Heartizan Way.

The most important thing to do is to have a plan, get some accountability and take action. Your plans do not have to be longwinded, they can be simple and even jotted down in a notebook or on your phone. That way your business work in progress can become a beautiful crafted finished piece and your dreams can be a reality.

HEARTIZAN - YOUR WORK IN PROGRESS

Never give up! Life will always throw you curve balls and your plans will never run smoothly. I don't actually like to set goals and in The Imaginarium group we call them intentions; this way you can never fail. I often change my intentions and I rarely goal set, however I do have a business plan. This I constantly add to and change but it is a work in progress too!

Use your phone and take photos of your journey, record everything! I actually started doing this after I went to a session at the memory clinic. I have tried cork boards, whiteboards, notes on my phone, alarms, note pads and numerous other ways of remembering things. Taking photos is the only way I keep myself organised (my style of organised) and now I take photos of not just my work in progress photos but my whole business journey.

Repurposing – time management can be a hard one for small businesses. I have been down the Facebook black hole of time so many times and I know Pinterest can be exactly the same, but you need to repurpose your content.

You can do this in so many ways:

- Use your content over all your social media – share those images.
- Repurpose your blogs and use excerpts from them, leave the links to and get your followers to read the rest. This will get more traffic to your website too.
- Download your lives from Facebook then upload them to your YouTube channel. Then you can share them to all of your social media accounts. I especially love to pin The Heartizan Headlines onto a Pinterest board.
- Take screen shots of any feedback, reviews and recommendations and repost them everywhere and the same with customer photos too.
- Go live straight from YouTube, then pin, tweet, share and add to a blog.
- Use Canva to create an image and either pin or share to Facebook straight from the Canva account.
- Surround yourself with like-minded people, get rid of the negative nellies! I know this isn't always the easiest thing to do but having a 'tribe of cheerleaders will help you through. They will also tell you the truth and are such a good sounding board.
- Try and keep focussed on what you actually wish to achieve. Don't get distracted (this is so easily done). As crafters, we are always trying new things but stick to the main points of your business plan. Review it every quarter, amend as necessary but stay on track!
- Lastly, and this is the hardest one, don't work every day of the week. Have some "me time" and spend those precious moments making memories with your loved ones. I have missed out on parts of my children's lives because I have worked all hours, but time goes so fast and they grow up in the blink of an eye.

CREATIVE CURATING

Curating is quite a buzzword now and it can be used interchangeably in many forms. In the creative community it means putting together and organising our products, stories and other content to use on social media platforms. Heartizan curates the home page with our wonderful creatives' items on display. However, for this chapter the meaning is slightly different. It pertains to selecting, organising, presenting and using our expert knowledge to help our creatives use a network effectively whilst sharing their content.

Heartizan has built up lots of great connections and this has helped to raise our profile on our main social media platforms. We have helped creatives to become award-winning businesses and we share how to do this on our Facebook groups. We have an amazing Twitter expert on hand who has helped us grow, Dylan Moore, who owns the Aqua Design Group, has curated a list of awards and helps us to under- stand Twitter. He also designs some amazing badges for the twitter awards too.

Pinterest and Instagram are both great platforms for creative businesses and if you take the time to learn how they work they will also help your business grow.

SOCIAL MEDIA AWARD INFORMATION

Heartizan is continuing to grow and what we have learnt on our journey is always passed to our creatives and the Heartizan Madmin Team. Madmins and creatives are scooping awards up nearly every week! This has been written to help all small business (not just creative ones) to go out there, find those rewards and win them!

AWARDS AND WHERE TO FIND THEM – SOCIAL MEDIA AWARD INFORMATION

Twitter is a great start and they have lots going on each week to help gain exposure for your business along with some fabulous awards for your businesses. Some national awards require an entry fee, or you will need to pay for a ticket to the finals, which is normally a black-tie event. This is a great excuse to dress up and network with other small businesses! Something we all don't do very much of, I am sure. You can Google the national awards and for the local awards just check out your local newspapers. Everyone has a story and as business owners you should be telling it, getting visible by being seen and heard. Awards are the very start of this, so set aside time to research and apply.

TWITTER

MONDAY TO FRIDAY

Awarding Woman in Biz

Rules: Follow @HealthyLondonUK

Use the hashtag #WomanInBiz between 6pm and 7pm every evening, post about your business and retweet all that take part.

The winner will receive a personalised badge, fabulous support and lots of exposure on Twitter.

TUESDAY

King of Award@ADG_IQ

Rules: Follow Andy Quinn @ADG_IQ and tweet about your business between 9am and 9pm using the hashtag #kingof

The winner will receive a personalised badge and will be added to the Royal Connection Group and will also be part of the Royal Connection website.

WEDNESDAY

Jacqueline Gold@Jacqueline_Gold

Wow - awarded by Jacqueline Gold (founder of Ann Summers) Rules:

Follow Jacqueline Gold If you are a female entrepreneur and tweet Jacqueline about your business using the hashtag #WOW

The winner will receive the WOW badge and be added to the Facebook Group.

THURSDAY

Queen of Award@ADG_IQ

Rules: Follow Andy Quinn @ADG_IQ and tweet about your business between 9am and 9pm using the hashtag #queenof

The winner will receive a personalised badge and will be added to the Royal Connection Group. You will also be part of the Royal Connection website and this award will certainly help you grow on Twitter.

Twitter Sisters Award

Rules: An award for speed networking for small businesses. You will win a personalised badge and gain more exposure on Twitter. This is every Thursday between 8.30pm and 9.30pm. Use the hashtag #twitter-sisters

FRIDAY

The Heartizan Handmade Award - Hand to Heart is for creative businesses and is every Friday between 6.00pm and 8.00pm.

Rules: Follow Heartizan and use the hashtag #H2H

Tweet about your business and read the instructions on the Heartizan tweet.

The winner will receive a personalised badge and a lot of exposure for your business through social media.

Sunday

Smart Social Award@SmartSocialUK

Rules: This award if for businesses that are smart with social media, tweet them to let them know every Sunday between 9am and 12pm Let them know what makes your business social media savvy!

The winner will receive a personalised badge and exposure for your business!

Small Business Sunday@TheoPaphitis

Rules: Follow @TheoPaphitis and @RymanStationery. Tweet about your business in 280 characters or less directed to Theo adding the hashtag #SBS. If you have a website add the link (this will increase your chances) and use humour and topicality!

The winner receives a personalised badge, are added to the SBS Facebook group and can attend the annual event to meet Theo and receive their award. You can also apply to pitch to sell with Theo's retail group and meet the buyers along with lots of other inspirational talks including Theo's fireside chat. I have learnt so much from the annual SBS event and I look forward to it every year.

TWITTER HOURS

Twitter can really help with exposure for your business and you can find lots of businesses that will to help you grow. The information we have given you will help you use Twitter more effectively, give your business more exposure and help you grow The awards and hours are subject to change but are correct at time of printing, even if they are no longer available these will give you an indication of what to look for.

MONDAY

7.00am #earlybiz

8.00am #ukearlyhour

11.00am #elevenseshour

2.00pm #bizhour #UKbizhour

6.00pm #womaninbizhour #wnukrt

7.00pm #smartnetworking

8.00pm #creativebizhour #mumsinbiz #mumsinbizhour #bizmum-follow #TNFhour

9.00pm #UKlatehour#gardenshour

TUESDAY

7.00am #earlybiz

8.00am #ukearlyhour

11.00am #elevenseshour

2.00pm #bizhour #UKbizhour

6.00pm #womaninbizhour #wnukrt

8.00pm #cupcakehour #craftblogclub #heartizanheartshour

9.00pm #tweetursis #SmallBizHour #UKlatehour

WEDNESDAY

7.00am #earlybiz

8.00am #ukearlyhour

10.00am #crafterscoffeeAM

11.00am #elevenseshour #UKcoffeehour

2.00pm #bizhour #UKbizhour

6.00pm #womaninbizhour #wnukrt

7.00pm #brithour #markethour

9.00pm #markethour #UKlatehour

THURSDAY

7.00am #earlybiz

8.00am #ukearlyhour 11.00am #elevenseshour

2.00pm #bizhour #UKbizhour #artisanafternoontea

9.00pm #UKlatehour

FRIDAY

7.00am #earlybiz

8.00am #ukearlyhour

11.00am #elevenseshour

2.00pm #bizhour #UKbizhour

6.00pm - 8.00pm #H2H

9.00pm #UKlatehour

SATURDAY

9.00am - 8.00pm #crafturday

9.00am-12.00am #UKgiftAM

9.00am-10.00am #ukweekendhour

9.00am-10.00am #ukgifthour

SUNDAY

9.00am-12.00pm #UKgiftAM

9.00am-12.00am #smartsocail

9.00am-10.00am #ukgifthour

7.00pm #womaninbiz #Onlinecraft #Ukcrafthour

8.00pm #handmadehour

9.00pm-11.00 #craftbizparty

HEARTIZAN - HOW TO WIN AT SOCIAL MEDIA

- Social media is constantly being developed and it can be hard to keep up with all the changes – find experts to learn from, they will all have free social media groups.
- Don't spam or drop your links everywhere. Use a scheduler and plan out your week.
- Tag people, businesses and collaborations in your posts. Don't just post about sales – engage your audience too. Ask questions and do polls.
- Use the check-in facility on Facebook. Comment as your business.

INTERACT AND ENGAGE

- Follow influencers – you can learn a lot from them.
- Stalk your competition – not to copy them, you can get ahead of the game this way and learn too.
- Build up relationships and connections. Go live and share your story.

- Nothing happens overnight (unless you are very lucky) just keep going and it will happen.
- Repurpose, repurpose, repurpose.
- Take really good images, use white backgrounds or use lifestyle images. Our mobile phones are ok for this but as we grow a camera is a good investment for your business.
- Join specific groups for social media platforms they can help you grow before your organic followers find you.
- You will find the right social media platforms for your business, grow those but still have a presence on the other platforms. You can link your Instagram account to twitter, use a scheduler like IFTT or buffer and just get organised. Sunday evenings are a good to plan post, pins and tweets.

THROWBACK THURSDAY - MY STORY

MY EARLY STORY

I was born in Stroud; Gloucestershire and I was the third child of four. As far as I can remember, I had a happy childhood. I was connected more to my dad and I was his little girl who got away with most things. I loved him so much and even though my memories are beginning to fade now, I do remember being curled up on his lap, watching the TV and listening to his heartbeat.

My dad had quite a tough life. His father died whilst he was young, and his grandparents had a pretty wild history! He completed his Army service and he was a middleweight boxing champion. He married a lady called Joan and they settled down at Summer Street in Stroud and later on they had a son called David. Joan was very sick during this pregnancy and, unfortunately, they both died. My mum was my dad's sister-in-law and in time they ended up falling in love and getting married. After they raised us more than a decade later, my Dad lost his beloved job when his firm and moved to London and he didn't want to uproot his family (at this time, my brother was doing his exams and my sister was in sixth form).

I got up to the normal childhood things, went to school, had boyfriends and got into the usual mischief a teenager gets up too. I used to run at my primary school, and I was good at long distance; this continued into my secondary school and on to an athletic club which I absolutely loved and was very good at. I had fabulous friends and I set my sights on joining the Royal Air Force. However, I met a man a lot older than me and everything changed overnight.

He came into a pet shop that I worked in, even though I don't think he had a pet but through my hazy memories I know he charmed me and asked me out on a date. That evening, I came home from work and my lovely dad was getting the washing in off of the line, my mum was at work and I don't remember where my siblings were. I was 16 and I had the world at my feet, excited about my future and I was a very happy soul. My dad hadn't been feeling too well and had visited the doctors that day – he hated doctors and rarely went. I asked him what they said, and I was devastated to hear that he had suffered a heart attack two weeks ago. He wasn't allowed to drive for six weeks and was off work for a lot longer, though he could go back eventually on a return to work plan. My dad used to run Mitchell Cotts in Stroud; he was a mechanic. We all used to go with him sometimes and I loved going down into the pit and looking underneath the lorries.

I told my dad that I wouldn't go out that evening, but he insisted that he was fine, and I should go on my first 'proper' date. This date was pretty special, and I was wined and dined in Bristol and I had the most amazing time. This was the first boyfriend I had who owned a car, he was a manager of a butchers and being that much older was very attractive to a young 16-year-old.

I don't recall the time I got home but as I walked into the lounge, I knew there was something wrong. My mum, sister and my youngest brother who was nine was still up and they were crying. I don't remember the exact words, but they told me my dad had died of a huge heart attack, but he hadn't suffered. I remember my eldest brother coming home and then the next few weeks are a blur to me. The funeral was surreal. I remember how packed it was with people standing at the back. I remember my beloved dad in a coffin at the front of the church and I remember his cremation. The heart I listened to beating had given up on us both and it was time to say goodbye to the only man in my life who just wanted the best for me and who totally understood me.

The next year is quite hazy in my memory, I continued to date the older man who turned into a dominating and abusive person who tried to control my every move. I could not look at another male of my age or wear pretty clothes and make-up. I moved into a flat with him and the abuse became much, much worse. A few months later I found out I was pregnant, which at 16 and in 1987 was a quite a shock to my family. My Mum found me a couple from her church who wanted to adopt my baby, but this wasn't an option for me. The abuse still continued, and I became fearful for my baby's life; this made me strong and I left the man who had continued to hurt and scar me. Being frightened had broken me and leaving was a release; I had hopes and dreams again.

At three months pregnant, I moved back in with my mum and I tried to get on with my life, to put this awful year behind me and to build my future with my baby. I went out with friends again; the isolation had been awful, but I was a fighter even back then and learnt to be happy again. I met a man my age and we just clicked, me being pregnant was not an issue and we connected deeply.

When I was five months pregnant, my ex-partner pulled up in his car after I had left work and talked me into getting into the car with him. He said just wanted to talk about the baby and would take me straight home. This didn't happen, and he subjected me to more horrific abuse and kidnapped me for nine hours; he threatened to kill me on the motorway and forced my head under the steering wheel so I couldn't be seen. The police, my family, my friends and my gorgeous boyfriend were all out looking for me. I eventually broke free, escaped and got home but this impacted on my health and I was in and out of hospital. I soon developed pre-eclampsia and my beautiful baby girl was born a few weeks early.

My boyfriend stuck by me and I moved into a Mother and Babies home when my daughter was a few weeks old. I met the most amazing women there and we lived a fabulous life, having fun and raising our children together. I recall this time in my life with the fondest of memories. You could only stay in the Mothers and Babies home for two years before they'd house you. Just as this was about to take place, my gorgeous Nanna died on my eighteenth birthday. My mum had gone on holiday and I remember my eldest sister visiting me to let know. I had been very close to my Nanna; she believed in me and supported me throughout my life. Before I got my new house, life got a little darker; the home was set on fire and I had to go to court for an injunction for my safety.

The last few years as a teenager taught me a lot of lessons and just how fragile life can be. I lived for the moment, I made rash decisions, I spent money wildly and I loved deeply. I became a mechanic, which I loved; the smell made me feel close to my dad and I was pretty good at it! The owner taught me so much and started entering me into competitions for trainee mechanics. I was really strong for a girl but with my little hands I could drop an engine out very fast! Unfortunately, he sold the garage and the new owner was nowhere near as lovely. He took me out of the competitions and he had me replacing tyres, water pumps and little easier tasks. He was rude and creepy and got far too close to me. I was at work one day and all the other mechanics were either delivering or picking up vehicles and I was given another water pump to replace. The owner came under the ramp and got so close that I could smell his breath and he told me how beautiful he thought I was and how attracted he was to me. He became very explicit and I froze in shock, I had no idea what to do and then asked me to touch him, which I refused. I ran out and drove my car to my partner's work. The car had been given to me by the owner when I had passed my test. – I then knew why. He was married with children and I didn't realise at the time that he was another predatory man. I never went back to that job, but I quickly found another one, in a forecourt shop. I settled into family life and time went by raising my daughter with my partner living our best lives.

We had got together at seventeen years old and our relationship started to suffer, and we also began to argue. We had been together for six years, but it was coming to an end. My cousin offered me a manager's job in his garage, and I jumped at the chance. After a couple of months, my partner moved out and I was heartbroken, but I threw myself into work. I had always loved art; I drew a lot as a child, and I started to make my own birthday cards and I sold them in the shop. I made friends with the people that worked there, and I started going out and having some fun. I was only 22 and I hadn't really had much fun in my life. I met a man called Jason who was from New Zealand; he was fun, kind and very charming. We had a whirlwind romance, but he was only in England for six weeks and then he left to go back home for his cricket season. He was a wicket keeper for the New Zealand team. We stayed in touch which was mostly by letter and the odd phone calls, there wasn't much internet back then, no apps, or Facebook or mobile phones.

By October, we were like love struck teenagers and we missed each other terribly, we had such a connection and when he asked me to emigrate, I immediately agreed. I have always grabbed opportunities with both hands, the timing was right, and I knew I would regret it if I didn't just do it! So, by early December my daughter and I packed up our home and our lives in Gloucestershire and we made the long trip to New Zealand. It was incredibly exciting, and I will never forget the feeling of elation and fear that mixed itself up in my tummy. I felt truly alive.

I arrived in a picturesque little bay called Whangaparao and I fell in love with it immediately. We moved in with Jason's parents and his brother, but Jason left for a cricket tour soon after I got there. It was a strange three weeks, but Jason arrived back just before Christmas and I soon settled in to live in New Zealand. Christmas Day was scorching hot and we spent time on the beach enjoying the sunshine. I have to admit; I wasn't keen on Christmas in the sun and our dinner wasn't like the ones we had back home. We settled in quite quickly even though my partner was soon leaving for another cricket tour! My daughter and I explored the gorgeous coastlines, went shopping and generally relaxed for what seemed the very first time since I was a child.

A couple of months later we moved to Auckland and found ourselves a lovely place to live, a school and a fabulous job for me too! I worked in a special school which took a satellite class to the mainstream school and I loved the teacher and the kids we looked after. Even though it was hard work I adored the job and I had finally found the career I wanted, and it was something that I was good at too. I trained with the New Zealand Special Education Service and I was ready to finally settle down. However, our fabulous start to living in such a beautiful country didn't last too long and reality hit us both. My partner was away a lot and we had to apply for residency which was a long drawn out process. Unfortunately, (even though I was granted residency) our relationship finished, so I met my sister in Australia, and we returned back home to Britain.

I have always been a person who doesn't give up, who doesn't brood on things and moves on quickly. This was no different and I was soon working in a home for autistic adults and another residential home for learning disorders whilst I completed a course for a diploma in business. We moved back into my mum's house and my youngest brother and I bought a car together. It was good to be back, and I was soon out enjoying life again. After my course finished, I was offered the manager's job in one of the homes and I decided to retrain and learn about autism. I was quickly promoted and I was made a manager of a brand-new intensive care unit for four, low functioning and challenging young people. I learnt so much, not just about autism but how to lead a team, about myself and where I wanted to be in life. My partner from New Zealand gave up his cricket career and returned to England, we tried once more but sadly it wasn't meant to be.

I bought my first house and life settled back down again but not for too long, as I met the man next door! I seem to be attracted to men with issues or unresolved problems and this was no different. I fell hard and fast in love and a few months later we were house hunting. I sold my house and I made a considerable amount of money from the sale and we bought a lovely home together. Not long after I was pregnant, and life became another round of hospital appointments, doctors and monitoring. My body struggled with pregnancy and I was soon on bed rest and had pre-eclampsia again. Though this was no surprise as it turned out the father of my baby was cheating on me with his ex-wife. I remember the evening so well. After dinner, my partner went for a shower, dressed up and he smelled great. I was told he had to go to price up a job for his boss, but I had my doubts as he had never done this before and being a builder, he never dressed up during the week, but he left and was gone most of the evening.

The next day at work, my deputy manager asked me what I was doing at the top of town the previous night and it transpired that my car was parked outside his ex-wife's house. I felt sick and bad memories came flooding back to me. Not only had my first partner been abusive to me, he also had cheated on me too. I left work immediately to confront him and even though he tried to deny it, I knew he was lying, and my heart broke all over again. The next month was just a blur. He moved out and then back in again and two months later I had a healthy baby girl who entered the world bum first and was absolutely gorgeous!

I had already decided to leave work and I was accepted on a nursing course at The University of Central England in Birmingham. I decided I needed to stay with my partner for at least a few years. My partner had three daughters and the eldest one moved in with us, so we became a family of five and a dog. Not long later I found out that he was an alcoholic and had been for the majority of his adult life. His daughter and I found over 50 bottles and cans that he stashed in the house. They were in my daughter's bedroom, in cupboards, behind the toilet and outside in the shed, they were everywhere. We lined them up all over the patio but strangely we never discussed it and life just carried on.

My nurse training was hard. I loved it, but I had to work at the hospital as well as my student shift, so I did very long days. We never had any money as it was always drunk away but I earned enough to pay the bills and keep a roof over our heads. I came home each night to a partner who had passed out in the armchair and usually a glass of wine spilled all over the floor. I managed to get through the training and I qualified as a nurse with a commendation. I had already been offered a job at the Psychiatric Care Unit where I completed my last placement. That relationship ended, I was a single Mum again, but I felt huge relief of being free and life was good again.

I later found out my mortgage payments weren't being paid, even though I had paid my half. I ended up having to re-mortgage the house and pick up as much overtime as I could, which wasn't easy to juggle with family life. I did manage a few nights out with my friends and eventually I found a new partner and initially we were very happy. I got promoted and a year later I found out I was pregnant, and we started planning our wedding. I became very ill and was admitted to hospital at five months pregnant with liver failure and an enlarged spleen. I was eventually allowed home on bed rest but not long after my waters broke, and my twin babies were born three months early.

It was a huge shock and my miracle babies had to fight to survive. My daughter arrived just after we got to the hospital, but I didn't get to see her, and she couldn't breathe on her own. I was then prepped for surgery as my son was not ready and needed help to be delivered, however he arrived without the need for a caesarean thirty minutes later and again was also not breathing so he was whisked away too. I was given a photo of them nine hours later and finally I could go the neonatal unit to see them. There was nothing that could have prepared me for what I was about to see. My beautiful children had wires coming out of their tiny bodies and they couldn't breathe for themselves. I was taken to one side and informed that there were not enough cots in the neonatal unit for two babies so they would be transferred out of county. My fiancé asked if they would survive the journey, but the doctor could not reassure us that they would.

They were transferred to Bath Neonatal Hospital a few hours later. My daughter went first, and we weren't allowed to go with her, so we decided to go in between them. Her brother was struggling so we stayed with him for a little while longer. My daughter survived the transfer and was doing okay on our arrival, however my son encountered problems and when he arrived, he was cold and blue, his incubator had stopped working and the medical team had to work on him through the night. I then collapsed with eclampsia, but I couldn't rest and needed to be with my babies. My son deteriorated for a few days but then he fought and stabilised but then it was my daughter's turn. She couldn't breathe on her own and for the next two weeks she became very ill. Cot space became available in our local hospital and they were transferred back to the neonatal together in the same incubator. My daughter continued to deteriorate and at six weeks old she went back to the intensive care department of the neonatal. They were now split up as my son was starting to improve however, my daughter could not breathe on her own for long and she continued to struggle. However, she started to improve just before Christmas and three months after they were born, they were discharged home.

My doctor knew something was wrong when my twins were born; he had tested my bloods from the hospital and at six weeks old he found out that I was positive for Cytomegalovirus (CMV). CMV is quite a common virus related to the herpes complex and to most people it was a cough and a cold. For pregnant women it is very dangerous and if newborn babies have congenital CMV (passed on within the womb from mother to baby) then the virus could be deadly. Most babies with CMV are born disabled with deafness, blindness and with a limited life span. I believe my children arrived so early that the virus could not take hold for too long and my daughter knew she had to be born. They were let down by the medical services as they neglected to take a second blood test which would have diagnosed the CMV, but it was too late for the anti-viral medication to be administered at birth.

We settled into a crazy routine of feeds, nappies, washing and the sleepless nights but we managed through it all and soon we had two healthy and happy babies. They were regularly tested for their vision and hearing along with developmental milestones and the CMV became inactive a few years later. When they were nine months old, I married their dad, but he unfortunately changed and became an aggressive man and controlling. I couldn't live with another violent man, so he was arrested, and we have not seen him since. Life hit rock bottom again and I eventually lost my house and had to move; however, I was pregnant again! I gave birth to a healthy gorgeous boy and he was my fifth and final child.

I returned to my nursing position a year later, but I found the shift work so difficult and my night shifts had to also include days, so it was time to leave and I found a part-time job nursing child within the youth support team. It was a perfect position for me, and I absolutely loved it! I was a Psychiatric Nurse specialist in a fairly new team, and I loved the new role. Life wasn't easy with three little ones and an eight-year-old, but we were happy and everything was calm for a change. This of course did not last and although I had given up on relationships the local village school was my next struggle. I had been placed on long-term sick leave too and life was really starting to kick me when I was on my knees already. I woke up one day in a large pool of blood and I was about to go through many investigations, tests and diagnoses.

My son did not seem to cope with school, he became anxious and could not learn the same as the other children. At five years old, he started to show difficulty with communication, distress and anxiety at school. He used to say that the classroom sounded like a herd of elephants – which was of course due to his sensory sensitivity. He was obsessed with water, so he used to run off to the bathroom during the school day and that was a problem for the staff. He couldn't help it. He liked Blue Tac too, but they took it away and he ended up trying to climb up radiators and shelves to get it. In the end, he was excluded because they thought his behaviour was too dangerous.

Unfortunately for us, we lived in a small village with people who had very little knowledge of special needs, so my son was quickly labelled as a naughty child. He spent most of his time at school either rocking under the tables, trying to run away or locking himself in the bathroom.

The headmistress, who was also the SENCO. said that my son may have Asperger's Syndrome, but she didn't follow up and he was put on high risk of permanent exclusion. Looking back, he was not helped by the school at all; he didn't do anything to warrant their treatment of him and there was a lot of missed red flags. I was called to school to take him home on many occasions as they felt they could not teach him, and they were just containing him. The headmistress now thought he had anxiety. However, that quickly changed to him being a naughty child with behavioural difficulties and they started to point the finger at his home life. I have been judged from when I was 16 years old and pregnant, then for most of my life for being a single mum with five children. I was certainly looked down upon in the village.

As a family, we were put through awful accusations and treated very unfairly; this culminated in being assessed by the social services who did not have any concerns at all. The fractured school relationship, which was at an all-time low, broke down completely when my youngest son was bullied so badly that he was hospitalised. I did not send my children back to that school. I was also very unwell at the time so I decided to home school my youngest three until I could find a more appropriate educational setting. My eldest son was being assessed by paediatricians and the Communication and Interaction team.

I found the right school and applied for my daughter and my youngest son. They had a unit attached to the mainstream school and Zack was accepted there but not until the new school year six months later. Both children got refused as they had no places, so I had to go to a tribunal to fight for them to get a place. My daughter was enrolled a couple of weeks later, but I had to go to another tribunal to get my youngest son a place a couple of months later. All of my children were in the same school by September of that year and my hobby business was about to take off!

HEARTIZAN - HOW TO TELL YOUR STORY

STORYTELLER – AN INTERVIEW WITH DOMINIC DE SOUZA

Dominic is a web designer, a graphic designer and is a stay at home Dad who looks after his wife who has Lyme disease, and has been through quite a long illness. He is also a novelist and a blogger from America. Here is his advice:

Blogging:

"The first thought is don't feel the pressure if you don't know what to say or if you don't have anything yet, don't worry about it. Not everybody needs to be blogging all the time. In fact, it's those people who have good contributions to make or are able to take existing or old ideas and then present them in a way that is unique to them and their experiences – those are the kinds of people who are able to create the interesting kinds of content that people are looking for. You don't need to be blogging every day, just start by doing it once a week and I think that if you don't have the genius for it, don't kill yourself starting out trying to blog every day. Maybe you try one or two or something but,

more often than not, good writing or a good content of any kind comes after a period of listening."

LinkedIn:

"So, for example, if you're not sure about getting on LinkedIn and you don't know why you should be there, think of it as a business version of Facebook where people get together to talk shop to talk about what they're good at, to reach out and network and help each other beyond just being friends. And you know, when you're building a network on LinkedIn, the idea is that you're looking to get to know a group of people reasonably well; network and connect with them regularly so that if an opportunity happens in the future, that person can have you at the top of their mind".

"The worst thing to do on LinkedIn is to start broadcasting and to start posting here's what I'm doing, here's what I'm doing, here's what I'm doing and not paying any attention to the network. It's far more valuable and more helpful if you start to storytell. In 2018, I was not taking LinkedIn seriously. I'd been on there for about seven years. I was connected to a ton of different people and I was trying to use it to get work and it didn't work. So, I just forgot about it and just used to do Facebook all the time and then I learnt that some people were taking LinkedIn seriously. It was becoming far more interesting. So, I realised that I wanted to get extra side work, so I needed to pay more attention to it. So, my goal was then to live on LinkedIn for about two weeks and try to get a sense of what made it special. The value that I got from doing that has been absolutely huge. Mostly because I didn't do any posting really. I just went around liking and commenting and really reading what people were posting. So, if you figure I'm doing that for like, you know, a couple of weeks, obviously it doesn't have to be intensive. I'm sort of an immersion kind of guy, you know, head and feet into something but go around reading what other people are writing, responding thoughtfully. You know, what you'll find is you start learning and you

start connecting with the kinds of people that you like to be inspired by."

"LinkedIn is all about opportunities. It's not the place you go to make sales. It's where you go to, to explore opportunities and to meet other people who might be able to put you in touch with other groups, other networks that you could've never reached on your own and then from there you might get sales."

Storytelling:

"Start trying to create personal, little one-to-one connections and start humanizing your network and not just relying on two profiles being connected, you know to represent a friendship. You will have new opportunities, new things to be considering. Or at that point you might start getting more of the validation you need. And that I have a particular story, or I have these particular experiences that have transformed me in a particular way and I'm channelling that into this activity. And I'm now realising there are people who would love to be inspired by this story, by these experiences, by the life lessons that I've learnt. And then you might find that blogging once a month or writing short stories, over a period of time will help you grow."

What to share:

"You fill a bunch of different roles in your lives, right? So it's kind of like a movie. When you think of the blurb of a movie, you flipped, you know, the DVD case to the back, or you're reading the description of a movie. It rarely just has the person's name. It says, you know, so-and-so, the financial banker is now faced with this problem. Right, or you know, this person who babysits for her friends or whatever does this, you're presented with a role, right? And that role is as it relates to what you're doing. So, you might be a mom, but perhaps that has no relevance to what you're doing with your store. So, you can bring that in. You don't have to maybe focus on the fact that you're actually a

college graduate in psychology who realised that there is a fantastic relevance to how you are making your quilts."

- *Show up consistently.*
- *Be the real you – people can sniff out fake a mile away.*
- *Take photos of your journey and record it – this will help you to remember.*
- *Share the good, the bad and the ugly.*
- *No-one may watch you in real time, there are always the replays.*
- *Don't give up, keep going, nothing ever happens overnight.*
- *Write down your dreams and make a vision board.*
- *Find people who inspire you.*
- *Sign up to Goalcast.*
- *Read inspirational books.*
- *Start blogging,*
- *You can repurpose everything.*
- *Deliver good content – be authentic – be truthful.*
- *Follow people who have the same mindset and goals.*
- *Watch TEDx talks – in particular Jules White, "There is no such word as can't".*

AFTERWORD - CRAFTOLOGY

Craftology is at the very core of what we do in our creative businesses but when we start or try and grow, we tend to get lost or over- whelmed and lose our focus. Creatives can generally turn their hands to most things, making lots of different products and trying to hit all audiences. Sometimes niching down and streamlining is more effective. There is so much to juggle, so many hats to wear, so much stress, so is it any wonder that most small businesses fail in their first year. If we trade for three years, we think we have made it, but we can just be treading water and not really making enough profit to become successful.

Heartizan understands how hard it is to get it right; we feel your passion and we really want to help you to make your business work. We have developed Craftology so that running a business is a whole lot easier and you will learn how to change your dreams into reality. It sets us apart from any other selling platform and it is designed to help all creative businesses start, maintain, grow and scale up. Heartizan has walked the walk, bought the T-shirt (handcrafted obviously) and been there and done that!

This book will help you to understand there is much more to a business than creating your products and posting them on social media.

Craftology will help you implement all the steps to running a successful business. We are so much more than a marketplace; we are a one stop shop for everything you need to know.

In the near future we will be taking our online presence offline so we can roll out our programme. We will also be holding events, workshops, meet-ups and maybe even Heartizan craft fairs. We will be launching an online magazine and starting a podcast to help share our creatives' stories, wins, new products, challenges and daily life. The very amazing and articulate Dame Vicki (Creations – Where Ideas Come Alive) will be recording the podcast episodes and will be helping our creatives gain even more exposure.

Heartizan is built by crafters for crafters and the Craftology ethos was curated by many creative minds, coaches, technical experts and people who were willingly to impart their knowledge to help others.

The essence of Heartizan is being part of a crafting family. It is the home of handcrafting and is the perfect place to visit, buy, sell or be part of an amazing team.

Amazing people making amazing things!

HEARTIZAN - USEFUL WORDS, PHRASES AND ACRONYMS, FOLLOWED BY A LITTLE BIT OF CRAFTY FUN

ACRONYMS & INITIALS

CTR (catch the replay) – this is generally watching back a live stream, usually on Facebook

CTR (click through rate) – on your lead magnet, blog or anywhere that you have a call to action button

IPO – Intellectual Property Office

HMRC – Her Majesty's Revenue and Customs

IG – Instagram

DTH – done to here – usually on networking ladders

RAOK – random act of kindness

FAQ – frequently asked questions

JCI – just checking in

LO – layout

NIP – new in package

PIF – pass it forward

TIA – thank in advance

TFFT – thanks for the tip

TT – technique Tuesday

PM – private message

DM – direct message

KISS – keep it simple stupid

PAS – pretty awesome stuff

GIF – graphics interchange format

PPV – pay per view

PPC – pay per click

CAPTCHA – completely automated public Turing test – to tell computers and humans apart

DBA – doing business as

POS – point of service

WIP – work in progress

SMART – specific, measurable, attainable, realistic, time bound goals

SWOT – strengths, weaknesses, opportunities, threats

BP – business plan

WEBSITES

SEO – search engine optimisation

Ecommerce – buying and selling of goods or services using the internet

Plug-ins – a software component which will add a feature on your website (PayPal, stripe, text box etc) so you can customise your website

Add on – will add a specific feature to your plug-in

Traffic light system – part of YOAST to let you know if your SEO is correct

Key words – self-explanatory, however you need to research these
YOAST – a plug in for SEO

WordPress – a platform to build your website on, there are plenty of others

Domain name – this is what you need to buy before you or someone else builds your website and idea

Caches – a collection of items of the same type stored in a hidden place

Clearing caches/browser – to function more efficiently, clear the cookies – which can generally solve problems clearing the data

Cookies – small files which are stored on a computer, used to carry information from one session to another

Spiders – these little critters help you get seen by Google

Hosting – stores a website or other data on a server that can be accessed over the internet

SOCIAL MEDIA

FOMO – fear of missing out – we do this a lot on social media and we end up not achieving our goals

Retweet – sharing a tweet

SBS – Small Business Sunday – Theo Paphitis on Twitter

Queen of – Andy Quinn on Twitter – The Royal Connection

WOW – Women on Wednesday – Jacqueline Gold on Twitter

Regramming – sharing an Instagram post, however you have to re-post

FLATLAY – an image used on Instagram taken from above

IGTV – Instagram TV – the lives on Instagram only last 24 hours but if you upload your lives, YouTube videos and videos to IGTV they will be there forever

Repurposing – using your new or old content on different social media platforms or emails. For example, you can write a blog and then turn it into an eBook, you can then use it in your emails or as a post on your social media accounts

Algorithm – a computer procedure (like a to do list) which takes inputs and produces outputs

Bots – an answering system that you can set up to reply to your messages

Live stream – pressing that button and going live on social media

Beta testing – asking your customers or business connections to test something for you (new product/programme etc)

Throwback Thursday – your first creations or makes when you first started your business

Fiver Friday – offers for one day only that cost a fiver

Top Tip Tuesday – does what it says on the tin, but it helps with engagement on your posts

Share the Love – sharing creatives' work

Tenner Tuesday – offers you have that are £10 or less

Madmins – The amazing admin that helps run Heartizan

Infographic – an informative post with text over an image

EXTRAS

Artisan, Creative, Crafter – someone who makes stuff Copy – text

Social Media Stories – these are useful for a snapshot and will reach your contacts – add copy to these

Comparitionitis (Jules White talks about this a lot) – don't compare yourself to others as it will only blur your own plans and stop you from moving forward

Repinning – using a pin that you have already pinned on Pinterest and repinning it to another board or adding copy and the pinning the image

Collaboration – to work together on a product, event or even on a live

Engage – talk to your tribe, followers, likers and audiences in a way that will make them want to communicate back so they are interested in you and your business

Accountability – someone who will make sure you are achieving your tasks, plans and goals

Organic followers – people who follow you without being linked to your tribe, family and friends

Sustainability – avoiding the depletion of natural resources – very important for businesses

Done is better than perfect – Robin Waite taught me this!

Mahoosive – just one of my favourite words!

A LITTLE BIT OF CRAFTY FUN

CRAFT – can't remember a flipping thing

Bunting and Business Plans

Phd – Projects half done Pro-craft-inating

Grants, glitter and glue guns

Knitting and knockbacks

Happy Hookers

To bling or not to bling, that is the question

Crazy craft lady

Get your craft on

Home is where the craft stash is

Crafting each day keeps the crazy away

A lady never discusses the size of her craft stash

You call it 'empty nest', I call it a 'new craft studio'

Crafting is my therapy

Creative minds are rarely tidy

Crafters gonna craft

Been there, crafted that

Make something awesome today

Given enough glue sticks I could rule the world

I craft therefore I rock

Craftiness is happiness

Make crafts not war

Eat, sleep, knit, repeat

Pinning for profit

Happiness is Handmade

Frustration and Follow Friday

HELPFUL APPS AND WEBSITES

Canva – a great app to help you to write creative engaging posts for your social media, PDF posts and so much more! The paid version is part of our Artisan Toolbox and The Imaginarium packages. The website has more features, but the app is great for posting quickly; you can even share straight from Canva.

HowToWriteBetter.net – nearly 2,000 free-to-view articles and tutorials on how to write for business, blogging, social media posts, even fiction and nonfiction books.

Buffer – helps to schedule your social media posts

Pic Collage – an app to create posts and images

Google Drive – a great resource for all businesses

Zoom – a great way to hold a meeting; this can be recorded

Vimeo – upload your videos so you can share easier (zoom for example)

Trello – an app to keep you organised

Todoist – an app for your to do list

Bitly – an app or extension to your website to shorten your URL links

Tailwind – A Pinterest and Instagram Scheduler, analytics and marketing tool

Designrr – a software programme for content marketing – helps to create great content with minimal effort

IFTTT – (if this then that) helps apps and devices work together – a great alternative to scheduling. If you set the Twitter option to retweet Heartizan you will grow exponentially as we have an army of tweeters!

Acuity – great for booking in appointments and daily scheduling

PicFlow – creates video slide shows for Instagram

StoriesAds – online tool for creating Instagram stories and vertical videos

AutoHash – uses computer vision algorithms to recommend the best hashtags to use

Repost for Instagram – Instagram regramming app

HootSuite – bulk scheduler for social media platforms

Video Shop – app to record or import video clips for IGTV

Mailchimp – email marketing

Some apps are free and most have an upgrade paid option. The ones we have listed are some of the apps and programmes that we have used at some point, however they won't be the right ones for all businesses, and it is always good practice to try out the free versions to test them first.

RAISING AWARENESS OF CHRONIC ILLNESS

Fibromyalgia - also known as fibromyalgia syndrome (FMS), is a long-term condition that causes pain all over the body. Fibro has many symptoms that tend to vary from person to person. The main symptom is widespread pain. Treatment is available to ease some of the symptoms, although it's unlikely they'll ever disappear completely.

Joint Hypermobility – Joint hypermobility syndrome is a condition that features joints that easily move beyond the normal range expected for that particular joint. Symptoms of the joint hypermobility syndrome include pain in the knees, fingers, hips, and elbows.

Arthritis – Arthritis is a common condition that causes pain and inflammation in a joint. In the UK, there are more than ten million people that have arthritis or a similar condition that affect the joints.

CFS/ME – Chronic fatigue syndrome (CFS), also referred to as myalgic encephalomyelitis (ME), is a medical condition characterized by long-term fatigue and other persistent symptoms that limit a person's ability to carry out ordinary daily activities.

Anxiety - is a feeling of unease, such as worry or fear, that can be mild or severe.

Everyone has feelings of anxiety at some point in their life. For example, you may feel worried and anxious about sitting an exam, or having a medical test or job interview.

During times like these, feeling anxious can be perfectly normal.

But some people find it hard to control their worries. Their feelings of anxiety are more constant and can often affect their daily lives.

Marfans Syndrome – a genetic disorder that affects the body's connective tissue. Connective tissue holds all the body's cells, organs and tissue together. It also plays an important role in helping the body grow and develop properly

ADD – Attention deficit disorder (ADD) is a neurological disorder that causes a range of behaviour problems such as difficulty attending to instruction, focusing on school work, keeping up with assignments, following instructions, completing tasks and social interaction

HSV2 Meningitis – an infection of the protective membranes that surround the brain and spinal cord (meninges)

Acute Intermittent Porphyria – Porphyria is the name given a group

of very rare metabolic disorders that occur when your body is unable to produce enough of a substance called haem.

Spina Bifida – when a baby's spine and spinal cord does not develop properly in the womb, causing a gap in the spine. Spina bifida is a type of neural tube defect. The neural tube is the structure that eventually develops into the baby's brain and spinal cord

Abuse – Anyone can be a victim of domestic abuse, regardless of gender, age, ethnicity, socio-economic status, sexuality or background. There are different kinds of abuse that can happen in different contexts. The most prevalent type of domestic abuse occurs in relationships.

Depression – a common mental health problem that causes people to experience low mood, loss of interest or pleasure, feelings of guilt or low self-worth, disturbed sleep or appetite, low energy, and poor concentration.

Autism – a lifelong disability which affects how people communicate and interact with the world. There are approximately 700,000 autistic adults and children in the UK.

CMV – similar to the herpes virus that causes cold sores and chickenpox. Once you have the virus, it stays in your body for the rest of your life. Your immune system usually controls the virus and most people don't realise they have it. Some babies with congenital CMV infection have health problems that are apparent at birth or that develop later during infancy or childhood. In the most severe cases, CMV can cause the death of an unborn baby (pregnancy loss). Some babies with congenital CMV infection have signs at birth.

Cancer - a condition where cells in a specific part of the body grow and reproduce uncontrollably. The cancerous cells can invade and destroy surrounding healthy tissue, including organs. More than 1 in 3 people will develop some form of cancer during their lifetime.

Addison's disease- also known as primary adrenal insufficiency or hypoadrenalism is a rare disorder of the adrenal glands.

The adrenal glands are 2 small glands that sit on top of the kidneys. They produce 2 essential hormones: cortisol and aldosterone.

The adrenal gland is damaged in Addison's disease, so it does not produce enough cortisol or aldosterone.

About 8,400 people in the UK have Addison's disease. It can affect people of any age, although it's most common between the ages of 30 and 50. It's also more common in women than men.

Anorexia - is an eating disorder and serious mental health condition. People who have anorexia try to keep their weight as low as possible by not eating enough food or exercising too much, or both. This can make them very ill because they start to starve.

They often have a distorted image of their bodies, thinking they are fat even when they are underweight. Men and women of any age can get anorexia, but it's most common in young women and typically starts in the mid-teens.

Raynaud's - Raynaud's phenomenon is common and does not usually cause any severe problems. You can often treat the symptoms yourself by keeping warm. Sometimes it can be a sign of a more serious condition.

Crohn's disease - is a lifelong condition in which parts of the digestive system become inflamed. It's 1 type of a condition called inflammatory bowel disease (IBD).

Pernicious Anaemia – is caused by a B-12 deficiency and is an inability to absorb the B12 that is needed for your body to make enough healthy red blood cells. It is a rare condition which effects around 1.9 percent of the population. It used to be fatal but is now treated with lifelong B12 injections, however if left untreated it can lead to severe complications.

Vitamin B12 or B9 (commonly called folate) deficiency

Anaemia - occurs when a lack of vitamin B12 or folate causes the body to produce abnormally large red blood cells that cannot function properly. Red blood cells carry oxygen around the body using a substance called haemoglobin.

Anaemia is the general term for having either fewer red blood cells than normal or having an abnormally low amount of haemoglobin in each red blood cell. There are several different types of anaemia and each one has a different cause.

Lupus - Systemic lupus erythematosus (SLE) – lupus – is a long-term condition causing inflammation to the joints, skin and other organs. There's no cure, but symptoms can improve if treatment starts early.

THANKS, THANKS AND MORE THANKS!

I am forever thanking my wonderful team. Without them, Heartizan would not continue to thrive. Their love and support are endless. They have all helped me survive the challenging times and they have shared in the highs of business and the ups and downs of my personal life. I am so proud of bringing my team together; they have made lifelong friendships and they certainly have each other's back, front and middle! The leads within Heartizan see the good, the bad and the ugly; they are always at the end of a Zoom, Facebook call or messenger and I will always be extremely grateful to each and every one of them.

Firstly, I wish to thank my Heartizan team of 'Madmin' without them our magical marketplace would not continue to grow.

Thank you to my partner in crime on the Heartizan shopping live stream. Dame Vicki not only keeps me smiling but she keeps me sane too!

The Crafters Display is our busiest group and was run by me initially before the marketplace launched.

This is now run by a fabulous team who help our creatives get seen by challenging them to go live and to help them start thinking about upscaling their businesses. It is a great learning resource and a fun place to hang out too.

Another big thank you to the Marketplace Team, our fabulous Angela Ramsden (Dolly Rocker) Dale Patrick-Evans (King of Chocolate and our only male 'Madmin' – god bless him) and Vicki (Dame) who all help out being the scenes. They all work tirelessly with listings, SEO and all things marketplace related.

My next thank you is to Emma Evans who not only keeps me organised but runs The Artisan Toolbox so efficiently with the help of our lovely Vicki. She also answers the page messages and directs them to where they need to be.

The Social Media Team are also amazing, Di Ward runs Twitter, Jess Lancaster pins on Pinterest and a fabulous team schedule them all.

A big thank you to you all for scheduling our creatives products and raising their profiles everywhere! Our incredible Angela Pickhaver is also part of this team and runs our Facebook Page with grace and tenacity, along with recruiting and training our new 'Madmin'.

The marvellous Dawnliza Lafreneire looks after Instagram and helps our creatives get seen by sharing their amazing products and using the best hashtags.

Heartizan will be rolling out our new programme next year and going to more offline events. These events will be led by the remarkable Vicky Bannister and also helps creatives in The Crafters Display too. She will also be organising us all at Kirstie Allsopp's Handmade Festival.

Our sales and marketing team is led by Amy Searle; she is amazing at shouting out about Heartizan and is one of our fabulous cheerleaders.

My newest lead is the totes amazing Mandy-Jane Gregory who runs our Heartizan Hub where any small business can hang out and show off their creations.

The rest of the team are just as awesome and work tirelessly every day to help our creatives grow their businesses; Carol Flack, Debbie Edwards, Fay Nilsson, Sue Timcke, Laura Jayne, Sue Bolton, Donna Haig, Claire Oliver-Gibson and all of the future and past 'Madmins' who have or will be part of Heartizan.

At the very start of my Cuddle Beds journey I came across a beautiful lady who totally resonated with me. Stacey Sargison taught me about Facebook Lives and becoming visible and she was the first coach that I worked with. I met some truly amazing business owners through her movement, so thank you Stacey for teaching me about JFDI (something I have always done even as a child) and for not listening to Jane down the road!

Next, I hired a truly amazing Coach and Author Robin Waite, who I spent a year with, learning about how to scale up my business and to earn my worth. He specialises in business start-ups, growing your business, attracting more clients and making more money. Robin, thank you for believing in me and being 'normal' and I know I was probably a big pain the arse, but I learnt so much from you.

The last and current coach I hired was for Heartizan and I had watched her on Dragons' Den years before I met her online. We were in the same Facebook Group run by a fabulous speaking coach Helen Packham, who ran a challenge that we both entered. I knew who she was straight away; I also knew I had to work with her to help Heartizan grow. This incredible lady teaches you how to win at sales with the art of human conversation and is the author of *Live It, Love It, Sell It.* Jules, thank you from my heart to yours!

I have one more special thank you to our tech guy across the pond, Ed Troxell, who always, shows up, delivers and engages!

Ed Troxell has helped a nurse really learn all about tech and we are very grateful at Heartizan to have his expertise on hand.

Two more business thank you's go out to Eleanor Goold, a fabulous copywriter who helped us write beautiful copy for our website and

Carlo Boschetto for his expertise on Twitter and for our wonderful videos. Carlo has been a constant support to me and both of my businesses.

Now for my family and friends, thank you to my brother Steve who has held my hand through numerous dramas and given me his knowledge, time, food and alcohol when I really needed it. You are amazing and continue to inspire me. I thank my wider family and all of my friends too. Sharon and Sharon, you are my rocks and without you I would never have gotten this far. Ruth and June too, even though I don't see you as much as I would like, you both mean the world to me.

Sharon Allen, you wonderful human being, I will always be in your debt for being with me from the start of my journey, for coming to every event, pitch and listening to me talk incessantly about Heartizan and Cuddle Beds, for staying up until the early hours sewing with me and for getting ready for whatever crazy idea I had next. You have always believed in me and for that I am truly grateful from the top and bottom of my heart. You are the family I picked for myself and I love you loads.

Sharon Hall, even though you have your own struggles you are always there for me too and have ridden this rollercoaster with me. You are one of my best ever friends from my nursing days and we share such fond memories of nursing, holidays and getting drunk. Boni Lloyd, I also have to thank you too, a crappy educational system started our friendship and I can't thank you enough for being there for me through the thick and thin. I really don't know where my children and I would be without your organisation, support and humour! Also, a huge thank you to Andrea Townsend, Cuddle Beds would certainly not be where it is without you; your nimble fingers and calm demeanour have been invaluable.

My heartfelt thank you to everyone who has been involved in my business journey – you have probably helped me much more than you know.

My last thank you goes to the very special people in my life who have seen the smiles, the tears, the frustration, the diagnoses, the pain and the amount of work that has gone into the last four years. Jaimee, Mollie, Amber, Zack and Jaycob, I love you so much and thank you for putting up with me whilst building my businesses. You all deserve a medal and much, much more. Everything I do is for you guys. Ethan, Aiden and Finley I love you all too, my handsome grandsons and one day I hope you read this and learn a bit more about your Nanna with a smile.

ABOUT THE AUTHOR

Chrissie Lowery is a single mum of 5 children and 3 grandsons, and she lives near the gorgeous Cotswolds of Gloucestershire in Stroud.

She has had a pretty colourful life and has finally settled down to be an entrepreneur, mum, friend and "Lady Lowery" of the fabulous Madmin Team.

She has had her struggles, challenges, highs and lows but she never gives up and she has found her place in the creative community. This has been one rocky ride and she has learnt a lot of lessons during this journey.

Chrissie's career started off as a mechanic. After lots of different jobs, she emigrated to New Zealand and worked with the Special Education Service, ran homes for adults with autism, studied business and then trained to a be a psychiatric nurse. After her training, she completed a mentoring programme amongst others, and she worked in a psychiatric intensive care unit. Her last role before she became unwell with chronic illnesses was as a specialist in young people within the criminal justice system. As a child she always wanted to be a nurse and during her options she worked in an adults' opportunity centre.

In 2013, she became unwell and the following year she had to give up her much-loved career with the NHS. The next six years have been the hardest of her life where she suffered many losses. 12 diagnoses later, she owns two businesses.

The Heartizan Way is not only the story of Chrissie's life and business career; it was written to hold the hand and guide creative business owners and show them it really can be done.

Gareth Watkins – Director at The Autumn Fair met Chrissie at The Spring and Autumn Fair had this to say about Chrissie:

"Meeting Chrissie and being introduced to The Cuddle Bed Company was a breath of fresh air. It's inspiring to see a new concept, with passion and determination.

Whilst participation with Theo Paphitis' SBS pavilion at The Autumn Fair was near the start of The Cuddle Bed Company's story, Chrissie's development and speed of learning is straight up impressive, and motivational to small business start-ups. Most of all, lovely to see what hard work and the right platform can provide."

The final words come from our functional and fabulous Dolly (Angela Ramsden from DollyRocker) who sums up Chrissie perfectly:

"Have you ever tried to catch a butterfly with chopsticks, put a collar *on a puppy for the first time, or carry sand in a colander? Well, that's what it is like trying to get 'Lady Lowery's undivided attention, for her to sit still and focus completely on one thing. I have never met a more driven person in my life. Her strength and tenacity continue to astound me, and she really is a truly inspirational woman and mum".*

www.heartizan.uk.com Heartizan can also be found on:

Facebook, Twitter, Instagram, Pinterest and YouTube

Chrissie's other businesses can also be found on social media and on www.cuddlebed.co.uk

Printed in Poland
by Amazon Fulfillment
Poland Sp. z o.o., Wrocław